THE EXONERATION PAPERS

SUE NEILL-FRASER

THE EXONERATION PAPERS

SUE NEILL-FRASER

ANDREW L. URBAN

Published by Wilkinson Publishing Pty Ltd
ACN 006 042 173
Level 6, 174 Collins Street, Melbourne, VIC 3000, Australia
Ph: +61 3 9654 5446
enquiries@wilkinsonpublishing.com.au
www.wilkinsonpublishing.com.au

ISBN: 9781922810915

A catalogue record for this book is available from the National Library of Australia.

Cover and internal design by Tango Media.

Printed and bound in Australia by Ligare Pty Ltd.

Follow Wilkinson Publishing on social media.

WilkinsonPublishing

wilkinsonpublishinghouse

WPBooks

"The prospect of an innocent person being convicted of a serious crime represents a catastrophic failure of the legal system."

The Chief Justice of England, Lord Igor Judge
(1 October 2008 – 30 September 2013)

DEFINITIONS

EXONERATION

From the Latin exonerare – to 'unburden'. In the context of this book's title it means stating that Sue Neill-Fraser is not guilty (Cambridge Dictionary); to clear from accusation or blame (Merriem-Webster). It is not a legal term but can be used to describe the effect of the quashing or overturning of a conviction.

PARDON

A formal pardon, issued by the Governor of the relevant state jurisdiction, allows the release of the prisoner; it is the equivalent of forgiven, and does not change the conviction. It simply forgives it. Inmates who insist on being exonerated do not seek a pardon.

PAROLE

A form of early release from prison (subject to good behaviour) according to a timeline determined by the trial judge, in which the inmate is freed under behavioural conditions imposed by a parole board. Failure to abide by those conditions can result in the inmate being re-incarcerated for the balance of their sentence.

CONTENTS

FOREWORD

Miscarriages of Justice are fought and won not just by the person who has been wronged, but by the dedicated team of people around them who refuse to give up until justice is served. Sue Neill-Fraser has such a team around her; from *pro bono* defence lawyers to a former prosecutor, from legal academics to a former Premier and Attorney-General, from social workers to a psychologist film maker, from family and friends to the 36,000 Australians who have signed a petition wanting the case reviewed. One of these people is Andrew Urban, a Sydney-based journalist, who is not interested in merely feeding the hungry beast of daily news, but follows through a story: unpicking, analysing and retelling the story in an easy to read, logical and enlightening way.

The Exoneration Papers – Sue Neill-Fraser takes us on Sue's journey into the depths of the Tasmanian legal system; a legal system that, in my view, has seen a miscarriage of justice occur and a legal system that seems incapable of righting a wrong. How can this be?

It is a mixture of reasons from the customs and precedents that form the basis of our justice system to the adversarial style of examining an allegation of a crime rather an inquisitorial one. It is the refusal of the system to allow for the re-examination of evidence that was said to be available with reasonable diligence at the time of the trial. It is the strengths and weaknesses of legal teams who are only human and, who in the cold light of day, no doubt wish they had done some things differently.

It is the desire to get closure for a family who have lost their dad. It is the want to get justice for the victim.

It is the desperation to get a conviction such that some evidence is minimised, some evidence is misrepresented, and some evidence is never disclosed. It is flawed forensics – just as in Chamberlain.

It is the exposure of a key witness who was left unprotected, scared, and vulnerable. It is the tendency to fall into the trap of tunnel vision in investigations. Fundamentally, it is the inability in human nature to be able to admit that maybe, just maybe, we got it wrong.

This is a story, however, not just about Sue Neill-Fraser, but about the collateral damage to those around her; people trying to help, challenging the status quo, and instead finding themselves the subject of the law. After years of long-drawn-out legal action, charges and cases have been dropped, but not before almost breaking the people involved, both financially and emotionally. People have had to sell their homes, move their families, and engage legal representation to fight for their own innocence and reputation, all because in some way they tried to help Sue.

The Sue Neill-Fraser case has been more about a system determined to maintain the conviction than a system looking for the truth. The sad part of this case is that it has led to an undermining of confidence and trust in our justice system. It brings the old saying to mind: *There but for the grace of God, go I.* How do we rebuild that trust? By admitting our mistakes.

Ultimately, we need a Criminal Cases Review Commission established in Australia, as it is in the UK, Norway, and New Zealand, to review the entirety of the evidence relating to an alleged miscarriage of justice without the confines of the law that requires fresh and compelling evidence to reopen cases. And we need a Commission of Inquiry into Sue's case to turn over every stone and to learn where things went wrong: how culture, systems and structures need to change to prevent the same mistakes occurring again, and hopefully to discover who killed Bob Chappell so that justice can finally be done.

While Sue may now be out of prison, she is not a free woman. She has the threat of prison hanging over her head for the next ten years. She is not able to speak openly and freely about her case to the press and she is still characterised in the media as "convicted murderer, Sue Neill-Fraser". Sue will not rest easy until she has cleared her name and is exonerated. Neither will we: her supporters, her legal team, and her family.

Lara Giddings
Former Premier of Tasmania (2011 – 2014) and Former Attorney-General (2008)

THE ROAD TO EXONERATION

In the first months of 2023, members of the Sue Neill-Fraser Support Group individually wrote to Tasmanian Attorney-General The Hon Elise Archer, once again urging her to establish a review into the case. The Attorney-General once again rebuffed the requests, citing grounds that cannot be sustained. She writes:

> *The separation of powers between the Executive, Judiciary and Parliament is an important cornerstone of our system of government. This means that Tasmanian courts hear and decide cases, independent of and without influence from, the government of the day. Similarly, the Director of Public Prosecutions, who prosecutes crimes in the Supreme Court and conducts appeals, exercises his or her functions independent of and without influence from the government of the day. This ensures there is no political, sectional or other interference.*

This view seems to be contradicted by the Attorney's own actions. On May 4, 2023, she intervened to direct the coroner to hold an inquest into the death of Jari Wise, a man who died after being struck by a car driven by his former partner, overturning a Supreme Court decision made just hours earlier. Asked if this was the first instance of an Attorney-General intervening in this way, the Justice Department said it "is not aware of a similar direction having been made". Yet reviews have recently been held in the NSW cases of Kathleen Folbigg's murder convictions and Bruce Lehrmann's abandoned rape allegation in the ACT, both established by the Attorney-General of the relevant jurisdiction. The establishment of an independent review by the Attorney-General would not constitute political interference. Rather, it would demonstrate respect for justice.

> *As you may know, our Government amended the Criminal Code Act 1924 to allow for a further application to the Court of Criminal Appeal in cases where there is further evidence that is 'fresh and compelling.' This provides for further judicial review of matters, such as Ms Neill-Fraser's conviction, and a Commission of Inquiry has not been shown to be needed or justified in Ms Neill-Fraser's case.*

This statement can only be maintained by ignoring the long list of outstanding errors which have not been considered by the courts – see Anatomy of a Wrongful Conviction. The Attorney also ignores the number of legal practitioners (among others) that have called for an inquiry over the years – see The Bleak History of Calls for an Inquiry/Review.

> *Ms Neill-Fraser and her experienced legal team took the opportunity to make an application under this new law. Ms Neill-Fraser also later made an application for special leave to the High Court. In both instances, the applications were dismissed by the respective courts.*

> *One of my duties as Attorney-General is to uphold the rule of law. This means ensuring that a case is adjudicated independent from the executive arm of government. Tasmania and Australia's highest courts have each now considered Ms Neill-Fraser's case in great detail. It is important that the courts' decisions be respected. For me not to do so would undermine the rule of law and the judiciary.*

This argument conflates the appeal heard in the Supreme Court with the application seeking leave to appeal to the High Court. In the latter, the High Court refused leave to hear the appeal; it did not hear any arguments on the ground of the proposed appeal. There is a long history of court decisions (convictions) overturned after several appeals were initially lost.

Public confidence in the rule of law is maintained only when such confidence is justified, while the above issues, plus a petition with over 36,000 signatures (as at early 2023) suggest that such confidence is not being maintained.

This book makes the argument – and provides valid legal reasons - that Sue Neill-Fraser is innocent of the murder of Bob Chappell and her wrongful conviction must be addressed. An inquiry would be ideal, practical and in keeping with legal precedent.

And there is another way to correct this injustice and even salvage some of the reputational damage. It was outlined by Flinders University legal academic Bob Moles, in a report to the Tasmanian Parliament, as was reported on 19 October 2021 on wrongfulconvictionsreport.org (the blog edited by this author).

"It is clear that the errors identified in the wrongful conviction of Ms Neill-Fraser would be instantly recognised as such by many of the leading forensic experts, prosecutors and specialists in wrongful convictions across each of those jurisdictions (*UK, Canada*). Indeed, it is the common practice in Canada for their judicial inquiries to reach out to experts in other jurisdictions to assist them. It would be quite simple and inexpensive to subject our reports to such scrutiny."

The reports to which Moles refers were written by Associate Professor Bibi Sangha and Moles, putting forward non-contentious legal principles which would provide a basis for overturning her conviction. This would seem a desirable way forward, ending the interminable stonewalling and the resulting loss of confidence in the entire justice and political system.

Says Moles: "In the event that we were able to reach a consensus that appealable error had occurred in this case, the procedure for its correction is simple and readily available. There have been over 20 cases in the UK where the Crown has conceded that appealable error has occurred – sometimes in cases where they had every intention to proceed with a retrial. Once the Crown concedes that the appeal should be allowed, then with the agreement of Neill-Fraser's legal team, they could make a joint application to the intermediate appeal court for a further appeal. The new legislation allows for a 'second or further appeal'.

In the 2005 Australian case of Farah Jama, the prosecutor, having realised that an appealable error had occurred, applied to the appeal court for an urgent hearing of the appeal. The court sat the next working day. The judgment consisted of a single sentence: 'The Court, having read the materials filed by the parties and having considered the submissions and concessions of the Crown, is satisfied that it is appropriate to order that the conviction relating to the applicant be set aside and a verdict of acquittal be entered.' We see no reason why the same approach cannot be adopted for Ms Neill-Fraser."

AUTHOR'S PREFACE

Sue Neill-Fraser was released on parole on October 4, 2022, after serving 13 years in prison (of a 23 year sentence) since her August 20, 2009 arrest for the murder of her partner Bob Chappell. Her parole followed closely the High Court's refusal in August 2022 to grant leave for her to appeal her 2010 conviction. A regrettable decision, as noted by Civil Liberties Australia (CLA), whose President Dr Kristine Klugman and CEO Bill Rowlings were "not persuaded that the judges, with all three of them winning their spurs mainly in administrative, commercial and constitutional law, were equally as skilled and experienced in analysing and comparing the evidence of forensic science experts and how the burden of proof might be – inadvertently perhaps – reversed in a criminal case."

CLA President Dr Kristine Klugman said the High Court video hearing was both "a legal disappointment and a presentation embarrassment to the nation."

Tasmania's court of criminal appeal had earlier dismissed her appeal in a 2:1 decision, also heavily criticised, as this book details.

In Vol 1 of Murder by the Prosecution, published in 2018, I report how this case came to my attention and how it became a focus of my research into other wrongful convictions. Originally prosecuted by then DPP Tim Ellis SC, her conviction was supported and protected in court by the next DPP, Daryl Coates SC ... together with the entire apparatus of law enforcement and administration in Tasmania, including the political leadership, the Legal Profession Board and even the Integrity Commission. This was all amidst many objections in public to the conviction.

Sue Neill-Fraser was convicted in 2010 of murdering her partner of 18 years, Bob Chappell, aboard their newly acquired yacht, *Four Winds*, on Australia Day 2009.

This book picks up the story of the Sue Neill-Fraser case where *Murder by the Prosecution* Vol I left off, awaiting the criminal justice system correcting its many well documented errors. Instead, the failings of the system continued.

A woman was convicted of killing a man who had disappeared from his yacht the *Four Winds* – and his body has never been found. We now know that on Australia Day 2009, the missing man had confronted the young Sam Devine on board the yacht, according to Devine's then girlfriend, the 15 year old eye witness Meaghan Vass, with whom he had gone on board looking for valuables. A fight erupted … blood was spilt…Vass left the scene.

The public rightly expects the legal system to take the utmost care when handling a case such as this, where there is no body and no murder weapon and only flimsy circumstantial evidence on which to build a prosecution case. The usual test for guilt beyond reasonable doubt must be rigorously applied, and all other possible scenarios clearly excluded before a guilty verdict can be regarded as safe.

There was no evidence that Sue Neill-Fraser was at what the Crown claimed to be the crime scene, much less when the murder of which she was accused was committed. That was simply not known.

Yet Sue Neill-Fraser's murder conviction has withstood two appeals and the High Court has twice refused to hear her appeal.

Those outcomes on appeal are all regrettably due to shortcomings in how they were addressed and determined, not due to the invincibility of the conviction. This book refers to it as a wrongful conviction, which I believe is incontrovertible, albeit in strictly legal terms incorrect. Indeed, there are several outstanding grounds against the conviction which have not been considered by the courts, including inadmissible submissions by the prosecution (evidence by the forensic scientist and forensic pathologist) and the judge's summing up, referring to a wrench several times as a possible murder weapon as speculated by the prosecution but never presented in court. Any one of the many errors identified by lawyers is enough to have the verdict quashed. In this book, readers will see the nature of these failures.

Sue Neill-Fraser and her family have vowed to continue the fight to clear her name. And they are not alone.

By early 2023, over 36,000 signatories had signed a petition wanting the case reviewed. Lawyers and barristers have acted pro bono in her case, knowing her conviction is unsafe. Flinders University legal academic Dr Bob Moles and Senior Lecturer in Law Bibi Sangha produced a research paper in 2014 detailing the many errors at trial. They conclude: "There is no proof of death, no proof of killing and no proof that Ms Neill-Fraser was involved in any illegal activity." Their work has had the support of eminent jurists and forensic experts in Australia and overseas. (The Hon Michael Kirby AC CMG, well-respected former justice of the High Court, wrote the Foreword to two of their books. The Hon Justice Stephen Goudge, a Court of Appeal judge for Ontario, and Commissioner in a leading inquiry into baby deaths had retained them to provide an expert report to his inquiry. In launching the above book, he said they were 'eminently qualified experts' who were able to elucidate thoughtful recommendations to policy-makers in all three jurisdictions of Canada, the UK and Australia.)

Sue Neill-Fraser's former lawyer Barbara Etter APM together with Canberra barrister Hugh Selby, prepared a detailed dossier cataloguing the many failures of the police investigation – and evidence withheld – which was tabled in the Legislative Council of Parliament in August 2021.

Tony Jacobs, Principal Crown Counsel & a Crown Law Officer for over 30 years, has added his detailed critique to the clamour for a review. (See *This injustice, the product of our Tasmanian legal family* chapter).

Those who like to claim confidence in the justice system and point to Neill-Fraser's two failed appeals and two unsuccessful applications for leave to appeal to the High Court, ought to remember that failed appeals do not indicate guilt. They sometimes just add to the damage of a wrongful conviction. Take the case of Lindy Chamberlain….

"A dingo took my baby!" became a derisive joke in the early 1980s, mocking Lindy Chamberlain, the mother who claimed to have seen a dingo leave the tent where her baby Azaria was sleeping, during a family barbecue one night at Uluru in the middle of Australia. The subsequent police investigation and her trial for the murder of her baby, Azaria, became the most famous case of a wrongful conviction in Australia.

Chamberlain was convicted of murder on October 29, 1982; her appeals to the Federal Court and High Court were both dismissed. In February, 1986, after the discovery of a baby's matinee jacket (on which her defence relied but which the police believed did not exist) partially buried in an isolated location, she was released. A year later her conviction was quashed and a Royal Commission ordered to review all the evidence.

Chamberlain is not alone in having had to fight through appeal courts and even the High Court or petitions of mercy, before clearing their name and having their convictions overturned – such as Henry Keogh, Gordon Wood, David Eastman, Andrew Mallard, John Button and others. It is to be hoped that Sue Neill-Fraser will be another.

To quote former NSW Deputy Crown Prosecutor Margaret Cunneen SC from her Foreword to my previous book, Murder by the Prosecution: "In the trials in which I appear, I hope not for a particular verdict, but for justice to be done. Thanks to Mr Urban's lucid advocacy, I sincerely wish the same for Ms Neill-Fraser."

WHEN THE WORLD SHRANK

The round-the-world honeymoon Sue's daughter Sarah and her husband Mark had planned was cancelled at the last minute when Sue was arrested in August 2009. Instead of round the world, they eventually settled for a holiday round the corner, at Tasmania's Cradle Mountain, as Mark Bowles told the author in this interview.

Fate seemed against them. "Seriously, for the first couple of years, every time we wanted to leave the state and had tickets booked, there was always a court hearing on, or something going down. It was so infuriating and quite depressing. It was like the television series, Lost, where they go to the island and the island has this magical power that didn't let anyone leave...." A bit like Sue's prison cell, perhaps; the world had shrunk.

At the time of Sue's arrest, the family lived in the hope that the case would be dropped for lack of evidence. None of them believed Sue had killed Bob Chappell. None of them believed Sue could have killed Bob. That Sue was capable of killing anyone. There were no signs of fatal friction. At the time, Bob and Sue were the new owners of a splendid yacht and they were planning to sail the world into their sunset.

Mark, a genial young man with a positive attitude, was hopeful that the charge would be dropped. "Yeah. Look, at every stage, we of course had hoped that it would be dropped, but to be honest, Sarah and I were from the start, probably the most alarmed and concerned about it all going wrong and far more so than Sue, I would say. To us, it felt like a generational thing because it felt like our parents' generation, all the boomers, particularly here in Tasmania, seem to have this complete confidence, including I'd say, Sue as well.

"They were like, 'Oh no, it's... there's all of these checks and balances and innocent until proven guilty and so on, and it'll definitely get thrown out at the next stage.' Whereas Sarah and I, we didn't ever have the complete confidence in winning that others have had.

"And we were alarmed from the very early days by the kind of language that media and others were using. So I think we were concerned from the start. And it was actually Sarah who convinced Sue to get a lawyer."

When Sue was arrested, she was in complete shock. It reminded Mark of a passage in Aleksandr Solzhenitsyn's ground-breaking book, *The Gulag Archipelago*, where he gives a vivid description of the emotions when arrested. This is how he describes it:

> *Arrest! Need it be said that it is a breaking point in your life, a bolt of lightning which has scored a direct hit on you? That it is an unassimilable spiritual earthquake not every person can cope with, as a result of which people often slip into insanity? The Universe has as many different centers as there are living beings in it. Each of us is a center of the Universe, and that Universe is shattered when they hiss at you: "You are under arrest." If you are arrested, can anything else remain unshattered by this cataclysm? But the darkened mind is incapable*

of embracing these displacements in our universe, and both the most sophisticated and the veriest simpleton among us, drawing on all life's experience, can gasp out only: "Me? What for?" And this is a question which, though repeated millions and millions of times before, has yet to receive an answer. Arrest is an instantaneous, shattering thrust, expulsion, somersault from one state into another.

Sue was in deep grief and complete shock, "banged up and couldn't have free conversations. So Sarah was her power of attorney. And she was in the middle of all of many decisions; who was going to be on the legal team, who in the media we were going to talk to.

"And we were young; Sarah was in her mid twenties, I was in my early thirties. We were making this up as we went. There's no rule book for this stuff. Although as more and more supporters came onboard, obviously we got more and more good advice around us from all quarters; legal, media, forensics.

"But I have to say that this has grown way beyond our family now, this is a big deal for a lot of families. Many people have been impacted. Jeff (Thompson) and his family, Eve Ash, Colin McLaren, Barbara Etter ... so many people's lives are being substantially impacted."

Not least the lives of Sarah and Mark. "Yeah, I mean, it has been a really big strain from time to time. And although I do remind myself that other people have tragedies in their lives as well, but I think that the difference for us is ours has been on the front page of the newspapers literally, regularly. So it's just dealing with so much kind of living in this fishbowl has been very, very hard at times."

That's the sort of ongoing pressure that can strain relationships. It can break them. "Sarah and I have a great relationship. We've got a lot of strengths that keeps us together. And I think what's hard is we both go through cycles where both of us might be feeling strong and engaged and throw ourselves into it.

"But then Sarah will go through a period of burn-out but I'll be okay, so I can then carry her and then we'll switch. I'll be really in a down period and she'll be okay, and she carries me. But the hard times are when we are both feeling in a really black place, we can't support each other, that then creates this negative reinforcing cycle.

"And we've been through a few of those where we're both in a really dark place, and I've never hesitated to seek professional help when I need it. I go and get counselling and try and work my way through it.

"Both of us have amazing circles of friends ... each of us have a handful of really special friends that we've known for a long time who just immediately dived in and helped. We had many friends that have done practical things to help set up websites, run social media, get involved in the campaign, that sort of stuff, so that was great.

"But also the other friends that were just there to listen to us whinge and whine endlessly for a decade. So I'm very grateful because I know I've probably been quite a bad friend to many of my friends. I probably haven't given them much attention to their challenges, but they've stuck with me, so I'm very grateful for that."

Mark feels lucky about the support he got from his workplace, where he works as an economist. "I was fortunate that all through this time I've had very, very supportive bosses that gave me what I needed, which was just support when I needed to disappear to court, that was fine. I got my job done and there was never any issues, so that was great.

"But for me it was, again, living in a small place like Hobart where I'd be on the front page of The Mercury coming out of court and then I'd have to go to some meeting about whatever. It was psychologically draining for me to be sitting there wondering what people were thinking.

"But in terms of how did I cope? I had both psychological reasons and also for just practicality, I maintain very strict silos between my personal and professional life.

"So I virtually never talked about what was going on at work. My attitude was work is work, and my private life is my private life, even if that happens to be in the papers that day. And I did that for me, I had to keep that separation."

Sarah was nursing at the time of the arrest "and she's done nursing and healthcare related jobs right through. I think it was much harder for Sarah than for me, because she had more of a public profile and probably more people would kind of ask her about the case at work. And so she couldn't escape it.

Whereas for me, people rarely asked me about it so I could keep a separation, whereas she was always being confronted by it and that made it very, very hard for her."

Did people ever express antagonism towards Sue, those who believed that she was guilty? "I can't really think of any instances. I suspect that if people thought that they kept that to themselves. And to be honest, that's another reason why I never talked about it in a work environment, because frankly I couldn't bear to listen to that. That would be very triggering.

"There were times where I saw on social media, people I knew making really toxic comments and that was very, very difficult. And I think what's driven us forward though, is to really break down the ignorance that exists.

At the time of the arrest, instead of going on their honeymoon, fate introduced them to a whole new way of living. "When this happened, it really took over our lives. It was sort of everything in our life and work was squeezed in around the sides and things like friends and hobbies just took a complete backseat. And it was extraordinarily stressful. But Sarah and I felt we had a duty to throw everything at it.

"But where we drew a line was, 'Well, this has destroyed the lives of two generations. We're not going to let that happen to the third.' So we decided that for the kids, we were going to try and protect them as much as possible from all the trauma we'd been through, and have a normal life as much as possible. The thought of my kids having to have all of that trauma of their grandmother being in jail, and everything that that would bring up for them, that was a sickening feeling to me for a long time.

"But to tell you the truth, what I learned over time is that kids are very adaptive. They adapt better than adults. And because it was, for them, it was just what was normal. Originally, it was Suesue lives in another place that they didn't really understand what it was.

"Then they started to understand that it was jail, and we kind of tried to give them a simplified story that basically something bad happened and the police made a mistake, and so Suesue has to be there, but don't worry, we are going to fix it. And most of the time they were kind of like, 'Oh, okay.' That was their world.

"In more recent times, and particularly with our older child who's very bright and very alert and from a young age could read, she was reading headlines of newspaper articles with Sarah's picture on it and stuff like that. So she was picking stuff up. And there were times where they went through a lot of fear. Very afraid of police, very afraid of being murdered, very afraid of that sort of stuff. And we've just had to try and reassure them that they're safe."

Coming out of prison to her family, to her grandchildren, was a "very surreal, emotional moment for all. For so long, Sarah and I had been … I reckon every second conversation we've had in our lives together has been about the case, and stuff to do with it. And always sort of talking about Sue in the third person. And now to have her sitting there at the kitchen table, it's a relief - and it's certainly not over. And I think for her, I think in some ways she finds this harder than being in jail. Because at least when she was in jail, it was obvious to everyone that there was a miscarriage going on.

"It's funny, a lot of people, so many people have said to me, Oh, we're so pleased for you and it's amazing and great. And I think people on the outside think it's kind of like, Oh, that's done. She's out. Great. It's party time.

"It's not like that. It's very mixed. Yes, she gets some creature comforts, like I made bacon and eggs for her this morning which she hasn't had for a year. Nice, but she's got to go out and face the world where probably half the population thinks she's a murderer."

The day Sue came home on parole, says Mark, "was a day I never wanted to happen in the sense that the vision in my mind was exoneration and walking out exonerated. And I think that was hers as well. So yes, obviously it's nicer for her to be out than in. In many ways, it's still bittersweet. It's been very mixed and for me personally, my overwhelming emotion was a sense of, I have to say a sense of failure. Because Sarah and I had put so much of ourselves into this over what was basically the majority of our adult lives, and we haven't yet got what we'd been going for, which was exoneration."

The case is not over, as far as the family and the legal team are concerned. "They're all totally committed. So they've all maintained their commitment, they've all stayed in touch. And for them, particularly Paul (Galbally, instructing solicitor), Robert (Richter, barrister) and Tom (Percy, barrister), this has become very personal for them as well. For them, it's not just another pro bono case. I think even they are a bit shocked at how bad and how nasty this got. And they're committed. And we're so grateful to all of the thousands of hours of support that we've had. That includes people like Chris Carr, Paul Smallwood and Bob Moles."

What's next? "I guess to be honest right now for the family, our main focus is just supporting Sue to adapt to her new life. That's our main focus."

THE ANIMUS OVERLAY

When I first learnt of the Sue Neill-Fraser case through the Eve Ash documentary, *Shadow of Doubt*, back in mid 2013, it seemed like a miscarriage of justice. A bad one - I say that because it was so transparently wrong by every metric. Any reasonable person seeing *Shadow of Doubt* would come to that conclusion. I reacted to the injustice and began pursuing the case with a view to prompting a review by a competent, independent bench. I expected difficulties, given the appeal had been dismissed and special leave to appeal was not granted by the High Court. (The reasons for the latter have nothing to with the validity of her case, but one of the most disturbing mistakes in this case: incomplete information provided to the judges.)

But I wasn't expecting the level of animosity that would meet the proponents of the Sue Neill-Fraser cause. It was evident in comments in *Tasmanian Times*, from those whose certainty about the conviction was often couched in vitriol.

After NSW police - at the request of TasPol - seized unedited footage from a Sydney production company in October 2017, the filmmaker, Eve Ash, felt "violated". The ethics of the action aside, what stood out to her and her colleagues was "the blatant intimidation that was on display". The work in progress was seized after phone taps (and research documents meant to be confidential) gave the police information that it contained material undermining the murder conviction of Sue Neill-Fraser.

Her innocence had long been proclaimed by legal teams and supporters, not to mention herself. But anyone defending her was to be treated with contempt ... and worse.

There was a sense of persecution about the police actions, she says, not dissimilar to how a police state might operate. From 2017 to 2018, the documentary team making the 6-part TV series Undercurrent (Ch 7, January 2019) about the Neill-Fraser case felt intimidated by Tasmanian police, the producers tell me, with phone calls to film crew including an editor, cars were followed, phones were bugged – including discussions with lawyers – hotel rooms entered, secret warrants issued for bank accounts, raids, documentation and film footage seized (in Sydney).

In April 2017, when filming Undercurrent, Hobart lawyer Jeff Thompson witnessed Meaghan Vass sign a statement that she was on the yacht with two other males the night Bob Chappell went missing. Four months later, Jeff was raided, then arrested by TasPol and charged with pervert the course of justice.

Police had accused Mr Thompson of attempting to influence a potential witness to identify a person from a photo array in June 2017. He was also accused of preparing a document outlining the evidence he would or could give for Neill-Fraser's appeal, relating to the witness' identification from the photo array. A covert recording device was installed in a prison interview room to record a meeting between Thompson and the inmate Stephen Gleeson. But the device was left on for two months, possibly recording other meetings, contravening privacy laws. Justice Brett also found that the warrant "which had purportedly been issued by a magistrate under the *Police Powers (Surveillance Devices) Act* 2006, upon which police relied to authorise the recording of the conversation by surveillance device and which would have brought the recording within an exception to the application of s 5, is invalid on its face."

It wasn't until five years later, on August 8, 2022, that the charge was dropped (nolle prosequi) before Justice Brett in Hobart's Supreme Court. Thompson was one of the figures in the long running saga of the Sue Neill-Fraser case who has paid high price for his good intentions, thanks to TasPol.

His barrister, David Edwardson KC, commented publicly on the wrongfulconvictionsreport blog: "Frank Merenda (my Junior counsel) together with John Munro (instructing solicitor) and I have been fighting this case now for some years. Finally when the Judgements are published everyone will appreciate how misconceived this prosecution was and why the conduct of TASPOL in the context of this case is so reprehensible. Every now and again there is a case which is so important and this is one of them. Jeff Thompson was just trying to help fight for Sue Neil Fraser's freedom. In return, his life and career was turned upside down by illegal conduct the details of which will be published in due course. Today is a very important day not just for Jeff Thompson."

Thompson's arrest was not an isolated incident. It was part of the animus overlay that was apparent even as early as the trial (demonstrated by countless examples of character assassination) and continued with growing intensity as the process of appeal moved ... inched ... forward. And it spread to the media.

On Sunday, April 5, 2015, Melbourne *Herald Sun*'s Andrew Rule let rip his then obvious prejudice: *IT was our very own Midsomer Murder, right down to the accused killer being a lady with pearls, a hyphenated name and splendid pictures of her favourite show ponies.*

Her name is Susan Blyth Neill-Fraser and she will maintain her position as the best-dressed and best-spoken murderer in Tasmania's Risdon Prison for many years unless a groundswell of support — and new legislation — frees her on a legal technicality. Just last week a serious newspaper devoted a full page to the proposition that the poor little "rich girl" got a bum steer from a sloppy legal system and unaccountably hostile police.

That serious newspaper was *The Australian*, the writer was me. "Unaccountably hostile police" is indeed an accurate accusation. Rule also repeated the later discredited police line that *She searched the internet immediately, wanting to know how long before a missing person could legally be declared dead. A little cold-blooded for a distraught woman hoping her man might turn up. She seemed more certain of his death, and hungrier on money, than she pretended.*

He even blasted her lay and legal supporters: *But no matter how many earnest legal wonks, cynical opportunists, noisy ratbags and conspiracy theorists encourage Neill-Fraser's loyal but deluded relatives and their social circle, this isn't a just cause.*

(To be fair, Rule changed his tune after his mate, the former detective and *Southern Justice* author Colin McLaren got onto the case.)

That sort of antagonism, visible in the way the police and DPP resist a new appeal in favour of protecting the conviction, turned a legal contest into a vitriolic conflict. That is dangerous and damaging to democracy, by pitting the well resourced legal system against the very people it is meant to serve and protect. It certainly feels that way to those involved and to some of us observers.

When caring, innocent people feel threatened or intimidated by the police for asking questions or disputing a murder conviction, you know there may be something deeply wrong about the culture of law enforcement in Tasmania. When what appears to be animus may extend to the office of the DPP and even the bench, you know that you are in a place where freedom of speech is under threat. Not to mention justice itself.

When I heard first-hand reports of such animus during hearings in front of judges, my dismay deepened. Such behaviour on the bench doesn't instil confidence as to objectivity. One observer was "shocked" that a judge who had earlier heard and refused Neill-Fraser's first appeal was assigned to sit on her next seeking leave to appeal, sitting on three hearings before having to be asked to recuse herself. It was the same judge who had earlier - in March 3, 2009 - signed the warrant to instal a listening device in Sue's family home.

PROTECTING THE CONVICTION

The friendly old kitchen table that I was sitting at, its polished brown timber top and edges pockmarked and lived on, had previously been privy to many long conversations at their home in West Hobart, between the late Bob Chappell and the woman convicted of his 2009 murder, Sue Neill-Fraser. That was in the days the long time partners (both with marriages behind them) were planning to jointly buy a yacht, a retirement dream. The days when they would share a drink during long conversations at this table; Bob liked a beer but also enjoyed wine. Bob would smoke his pipe, he liked to cook. Life was normal.

Long time family friend Bob Martyn recalls in an affidavit (intended for the investigators of the allegations of her murdering Bob Chappell) how he first met Sue at a social function in Hobart in 1974, but had no further contact with her until 1991, when he was arranging riding lessons for his daughter Penelope with Sue's horses. He found himself speaking to the woman he had met at that social do in 1974.

He soon came across Sue again at the Talaria Ski Club at Ben Lomond, where she was a weekend visitor. Coincidentally, he had met Bob Chappell at the Wellington Ski Club, also in 1974.

Some time later, Sue, by then divorced with grown up children, began a relationship with Bob Chappell, also divorced with grown up children, and they all began to see more of each other at barbecues and dinner parties. They had a common interest in sailing, Sue and Bob M both owning modest sized yachts, and Martyn carried out some repairs on Sue's 26 foot *la Bacquet*. (When she was released on parole in October 2022, Sue had not been on the water in a yacht since Australia Day 2009, when she left Bob tinkering below deck on *Four Winds.* Shortly after her release in 2022, friends took her sailing for a day. She told them it was one of the best days of her life.)

Ski clubs and dinner parties were the kind of middle class social networks in which Sue and her new partner mixed with friends like Bob Martyn, an employee of the Tasmanian Hydro-Electric commission for many years. Martyn and Neill-Fraser even became business partners in the mid 90s as directors of a property development company with the purchase of a 5 acre block of land in Brighton and subdividing it.

Bob Chappell, a respected physicist at Hobart Hospital, was, unlike Sue, "irascible, slightly eccentric and he didn't like it when anyone disagreed with him." Bob Martyn thought of Sue as kind and caring, "although sometimes vague and would often jump from topic to topic in the conversation. It was often hard to ask her a question without becoming confused as to where she was going with the conversation."

But Bob and Sue had "a loving if unusual relationship. They were never physically expressive in public, and didn't express any kind of affection towards each other in public such as cuddling. I found their relationship to be based more on their love of having intellectual conversations," thought Bob Martyn.

Back then, when life was normal, Sue's eldest daughter Sarah and her husband Mark Bowles were planning their round the world honeymoon, destined to be cancelled at the last minute, at considerable emotional and financial cost when Sue was arrested, on August 20, 2009 ...

That was then. This was Monday, August 20, 2018, the ninth anniversary of Sue's arrest. By a cruel coincidence, it was also the day that yet another set of hearings was supposed to begin at the Supreme Court, off Hobart's Salamanca Place, a 10 minute drive from where I sat in Sarah and Mark Bowles' home. Sue was seeking leave to appeal her conviction under new legislation that made it possible, following the first appeal in 2012 (refused) and the subsequent seeking leave to appeal to the High Court (refused). Sue had been denied bail and was incarcerated on her arrest.

The yacht of their dreams, *Four Winds*, had been sold for a relatively paltry $50,000 (a quarter of what they paid for it) at an auction with only one bidder. It had been built with a special hull comprising six (originally seven) watertight bulkheads at some expense, to withstand icy Antarctic conditions for charter clients. It is no ordinary yacht.

The shrivelled amount left from the sale for Sue's daughters Sarah and Emma after costs and sharing with Bob's estate, had long ago been spent. The legal fight had begun right after the 2010 trial. In 2011, the Court of Criminal Appeal refused her appeal and in 2012 the High Court refused leave to appeal. (Both decisions are flawed; for the High Court, see Could the Jury Have Got It Wrong? For the CCA critique, see *Murder by the Prosecution Vol 1*.)

In 2013 the State of Tasmania was given another chance to attend to what was clearly an unsafe conviction, as I reported in *Murder by the Prosecution Vol 1*. In brief: The eminent Melbourne

KC Robert Richter (with co-signatory barrister Greg Barns SC) wrote to then Attorney General Brian Wightman on August 2, concerned that Sue Neill-Fraser had been wrongly convicted, saying "might we respectfully suggest that the way forward is for the Government to set up an Inquiry (under the *Commissions of Inquiry Act 1995*), chaired by a highly respected, experienced criminal lawyer, such as Damien Bugg AM KC (from Tasmania) or the Hon Frank Vincent AO KC (from Victoria), to report to the Government upon the safety or lack thereof with respect to Ms Neill-Fraser's conviction." He continued; "...we are quietly confident that a Commissioner would report to the Government that the problems are so significant that it will be appropriate for you, as Attorney, to apply to the Court of Criminal Appeal, using the findings and evidence from the Inquiry, for the conviction to be quashed and for either a verdict of not guilty to be entered, or an order that there be a retrial."

This approach, argued Richter, would save the Court of Criminal Appeal from having to spend a lot of time on an evaluation of additional, new and fresh evidence in its limited context - a task which, in our submission is best carried out in an investigatory and non-adversarial forum..."

The Attorney General did not take any action and Sue Neill-Fraser stayed stuck in prison - with no real hope of rescue. Her next window of opportunity came with the introduction of new legislation in 2015, allowing her a further right to appeal.

Her then (2018/19) legal team firmly believed she had been wrongly convicted and were working pro bono; Melbourne based Paul Galbally of the famous Galbally family of lawyers, and Perth based Tom Percy KC. It was also a day that Galbally was in court in Melbourne, representing Cardinal Pell in his high profile defence against charges of sexual assault against two boys in St Patrick's Cathedral in the 1990s. Cardinal Pell, committed to stand trial on May 1, 2018, was found guilty, appealed and lost and took his case to the High Court, which on April 7, 2020, acquitted him in a 7:0 decision. He had spent 400 days in prison,

But for Sue Neill-Fraser and her family and her supporters, as they watched the Pell case move through the courts (as did the rest of Australia) the wheels of justice seemed to be square. And ominous....

Sarah, Anne (a family friend) and I were drinking tea, that solace for all occasions. The old kitchen table was an extension to a larger one, the two forming a spacious family table and conversation/socialising platform connecting kitchen, dining and play spaces for Sue's grandchildren. One (in a sparkling tutu) and the younger one were in the adjoining living room/play room polishing off a tray of fresh fruit and lamingtons. Pippa the coal black kitten was sneaking onto the table until he was discouraged by a spray of water.

The far end of the table was piled high with giant white plastic covered hard cased folders, the kind lawyers carry to court. Sarah had dragged them out, still looking for some piece of information that could guarantee a successful appeal and the release of her mum from The Mary Hutchinson Women's Prison at the Risdon prison complex in Hobart. Suesue, as her little kiddies called their unfamiliar grandma, had never taken them for outings, never played with them, never sat around their Christmas tree. Sue's toddler granddaughter had visited her in prison, but the visits had to be abandoned when she got older and was upset by the security rigmarole.

The hearing had been put back a day to the Tuesday to accommodate the jury verdict not yet delivered in a murder trial presided over by Justice Brett in Launceston. Sue's appeal hearing was also his case. I had flown in from Sydney on Sunday night, my fifth trip to Hobart (since October 2017, including the week that the hearings were deferred in June 2018) for the purpose of attending these hearings*. The delays were stressful for everyone, especially of course for Sue, incarcerated and isolated, fighting depression and despair. She had said to Sarah in a phone call from prison five years earlier how she could hardly comprehend the enormity of what had been done to her - accused and convicted of murdering her beloved Bob. And what did happen to him?

One of the big white folders contained a simple manila folder stuffed with papers relating to *Four Winds.* David Tanner, an old friend of Bob and Sue, had been trying to find out where *Four Winds* might have been prior to arriving at the marina in Queensland, where Sue and Bob took possession. Could the yacht have come in from a foreign port... perhaps carrying drugs, which had been hidden somewhere on board for retrieval later? It was a known strategy by drug smugglers. (See *The Missed Clues in Her Stat Dec*) The incoming boat may have been cleared in those less scrutinised days of 2008, but the hidden drugs had to be safely removed when nobody was watching. What safer than in the hands of new owners, in the distant port of Hobart? (See below)

The way *Four Winds* had been found at dawn on Australia Day 2009, sitting low in the water, her bow almost level with the surface of the Derwent, carpet squares disturbed, panels moved, it could be interpreted as a boat having been burgled for something hidden. Maybe found. But the point of David's investigation was not to prove anything so much as to explore whether there was a possibility of that scenario gaining more traction. Perhaps add another element that would establish reasonable doubt ... perhaps even new evidence. Too late, perhaps, but there was no knowing where this case would end up.

As it is the owner who has to make the request, David had enlisted the help of *Four Winds'* new owner since the trial, Chris Smith, in seeking the information from Australian Border Force.

But then, as always, our conversation rounded back to the many flaws in the trial and the lack of thoroughness in the police investigation. We were rehashing old ground. But the conversation was also fired by the pending charges of perverting justice that were hanging over local solicitor Jeff Thompson and Karen Keefe, a prisoner who had befriended Sue.

A bench of independent appeal judges, preferably from the mainland, would find - in our shared opinion - such grave errors of law in the trial that it would damage the reputations of all those involved.

I listed some of the most egregious errors, as identified by legal academic Dr Bob Moles, in Murder by the Prosecution Volume 1, (Wilkinson Publishing, August 2018). Moles points out that:

> *"The evidence given to the court by **the forensic scientist** was totally **inadmissible.** This error warrants the conviction being set aside."*
>
> *"The evidence given to the court by **the forensic pathologist** was totally **inadmissible.** This error warrants the conviction being set aside."*

*"**The prosecution address** to the jury was in breach of the legal rules and prosecution guidelines, and was **seriously prejudicial**. This error warrants the conviction being set aside."*

*"**The judge's summing up** was in breach of legal rules and was **seriously prejudicial**. This error warrants the conviction being set aside."*

But there was a fundamental problem with the conviction that on its own was screaming for attention: the rule concerning convictions in circumstantial cases had been broken. Not only was it a case of circumstantial evidence - it was a case without a body, never mind a murdered body. Ironically, two years after then Justice Blow delivered his summary to the jury in the Sue Neill-Fraser trial, he presided over another murder trial (R v Smart) where the evidence was also purely circumstantial. Blow was by then Chief Justice.

In that case, the circumstances involved an assault causing death. There is no doubt the accused was involved in some form of assault, but there were two potential victims and the question was whether the death of one could be attributed to the actions of the accused. The Chief Justice went through the evidence carefully, and determined that none of the evidence was sufficient to exclude the possibility that the injuries causing death were caused by another and not Smart, the accused. Therefore under the rules relating to circumstantial cases, it could not be established that the evidence was such as to be consistent with the guilt of the accused, and with no other rational explanation consistent with his innocence. Smart gained an acquittal on the murder charge.

Clearly, if there was any other rational explanation for Bob Chappell's disappearance and possible death other Sue Neill-Fraser killing him, she was wrongfully convicted.

Back then, on the evening of Australia Day 2009 in Hobart, the blustery wind was calming down and the fine day was turning into a balmy summer night. The wind dropped by midnight. Sue's mother Helen had earlier set out for an 80th birthday party at a friend's house. Her daughter's splendid new yacht, *Four Winds*, was moored some 500 metres offshore in full view from the front windows of her house on Marieville Esplanade. By early next morning, *Four Winds* would be taking on water and her daughter's partner, Bob, was missing from the yacht.

Marieville Esplanade runs along the Sandy Bay foreshore towards Battery Point at the northern end and takes in the Sandy Bay Yacht Club and Rowing Club.

The Sandy Bay Regatta had been the big event of the day and post Regatta celebrations mixed and mingled with Year of the Ox Chinese New Year excitement. Thousands of people were milling around or attending functions all along the Derwent.

With Daylight Saving, it was still quite light shortly after 9, when Helen got home; the Esplanade was still lined with cars. By the early hours of January 27, the revelry was turning into drunken brawls in the pubs and clubs and the police were out in force. After brief calls to her daughters Sarah and Emma soon after 9pm, Helen went to sleep blissfully unaware that her daughter Sue, who had gone ashore and left her partner Bob on the yacht earlier in the day - would never see him again.

Sue and Bob, both with grown up children, had been together for over 18 years. Their yacht was the culmination of a dream; they had sailed it down from Queensland just before Christmas, merely weeks before fate sunk their dream.

The missing Bob Chappell was presumed murdered and Sue Neill-Fraser became the prime murder suspect in the police investigation, although police had found no direct evidence to connect her to any murder. At the trial, the prosecution put forward that Sue, after going ashore earlier, had returned to the yacht to murder Bob, possibly with a wrench, and disposed of his body by putting it into their dinghy and dumping it (weighed down by a fire extinguisher) somewhere in the Derwent. Without a body and without a wrench, the jury relied on the prosecutor to flesh out what was unknown and unproven.

Perhaps Sue and Bob had acted unwittingly as drug couriers when they brought *Four Winds* from Queensland to Hobart just weeks earlier. Perhaps something had remained hidden on board. With its dinghy absent, it may have suggested to anyone watching the yacht that it was unattended - an ideal opportunity to board and search for the hidden item/s. Surprised to find Bob on board, the stranger/s may have felt threatened and panicked.

(On October 14, 2010, the day before the jury was to hand down its verdict, the AFP announced it had conducted a major drug bust worth $160 million involving a similar yacht at the Scarborough Marina where *Four Winds* had been purchased the year before.)

It is entirely possible that partying youths celebrating Australia Day and the Regatta on a nearby yacht boarded Four Winds, with or without malice, and a scuffle broke out, an accident turned nasty and people panicked. The DNA of the then 15 year old homeless girl, Meaghan Vass, found on the deck proves that at least one youth had been on the yacht.

It is also entirely possible that there were two separate individuals or groups who boarded *Four Winds* that afternoon, after Sue Neill-Fraser took the dinghy ashore around 2.30pm. The grey dinghy reported alongside at 3.55pm may have delivered the first (see The Abandoned Dinghy) and the youths may have followed some time later, possibly under cover of darkness. This scenario gains credibility when considered in the light of Sue Neill-Fraser's stat dec, in which she describes damage and violence done to the yacht. The apparent search for something fits the scenario that someone was looking for something (flooring removed), while the youths may have been in party mode, perhaps looking for alcohol and items to steal.

In February 2018, the 6-part TV series, *Undercurrent* (7 Network), produced by Eve Ash and CJZ Productions, made its debut. Former Melbourne homicide detective and author Colin McLaren had worked on the series and published his own book, *Southern Justice* (Hachette) at around the same time. Meaghan Vass, in the company of two men, had been aboard. She witnessed what went wrong - and fled the scene.

This was confirmed by Meaghan Vass herself in an interview on *60 Minutes* (Channel 9, Sunday, March 10, 2019 – see transcript page 55).

Our hope that August 2018 day sitting around the old family kitchen table was to hear the leave to appeal granted and the full court of appeal overturn the conviction, to have Sue released, the grandchildren united with Suesue and the end of this nightmare. But we knew that a successful appeal would be a profound embarrassment for Tasmania's legal system, not least the current Chief Justice Alan Blow, Sue's trial judge in 2010.

The central issue of the murder charge had become overgrown with the weeds of obfuscation from the start. But it became more serious when Tasmania Police took unprecedented action to charge Hobart solicitor Jeff Thompson with perverting justice. Thompson, along with author Colin McLaren, was working on Eve Ash's production of the TV series, *Undercurrent*, (Seven Network). Ash had made the documentary *Shadow of Doubt*.

Police alleged that Thompson deliberately influenced Stephen Gleeson (in prison on unrelated charges) and prejudiced photographic evidence "with intent to influence his identification". Additionally, he was charged with "intent to obstruct, pervert, prevent or defeat the due course of justice" in relation to Neill-Fraser's seeking leave to appeal, and "prepared a document outlining the evidence that he would or could give for the said application".

Thompson strenuously denied both charges. His case was repeatedly deferred as the Neill-Fraser case dragged on into 2019. After five years of delays, the DPP on August 8, 2022, finally dropped the charges entering a *nolle prosequi*. There was little choice, given that Justice Brett found the police had acted illegally conducting surveillance of Thompson when he visited Risdon Prison. The covert recording device was left switched on -illegally - for two months in the meeting room. Brett wrote in his reasons that his "conclusion followed from my determination that the warrant which had purportedly been issued by a magistrate under the Police Powers (Surveillance Devices) Act 2006, upon which police relied to authorise the recording of the conversation by surveillance device and which would have brought the recording within an exception to the application of s 5, is invalid on its face."

That decision led to an investigation into the police action, albeit (controversially) at the request of TasPol itself. It was announced in early September 2022, to be handled by former Solicitor General, Michael O'Farrell. It didn't escape the public's attention that in 2017, while acting in that role, O'Farrell expressed confidence in Tasmania Police and its ability to investigate matters in the Neill-Fraser case. "Concerns were raised"... and "fears were flagged" reported the Hobart Mercury.

But that came later. On Thursday, August 23, 2018, the third day of the 'final' hearings before Justice Brett was to consider his verdict on Sue Neill-Fraser's quest for an appeal, was set aside for counsel to make their final oral submissions to the judge. Justice Brett was not available the day after, Friday August 24. The deadline was 4pm on Thursday August 23. Tom Percy KC estimated he would need about two hours for his submission, and adhered to it. Darryl Coates SC estimated - ominously - that he would need about three hours. Mr Coates had already shown the court his unhurried, laborious style (to put it kindly) punctuating his address to the judge with frequent pauses and reassessed statements. After exceeding three hours and approaching the 4pm deadline, Justice Brett asked him to estimate how much longer he would need.

This session was scheduled to be the last of the hearings, a major milestone in the long running saga. I was seated behind DPP Coates alongside Sarah, Emma and other family supporters. We held our collective breath. Mr Coates looked quizzically at his younger junior, Jack Shapiro and said he would need 45 minutes to an hour or so. As this could not be accommodated, the hearings had to be adjourned yet again, to the following Friday, August 31, to be held in Launceston where Justice Brett's court was in session on other matters.

The public gallery, full to the back seats, filed out of court whispering angrily to each other, condemning the delay and questioning why it had turned out this way. The general consensus was that had it been a ploy to frustrate the process, and if so, disgraceful. And cruel. The grumbling continued over drinks and snacks at the Irish Murphy's pub a block away from the supreme court. I ordered a stout to match my dark brown mood.

I do not intend to fill these pages with the many details of the submissions (they run to several hundred pages of transcripts), but it is crucial to an understanding of the central and essential conflict between the parties: 'the Applicant' Sue Neill-Fraser and the Respondent, the State (of Tasmania).

Counsel had already delivered to Justice Brett their arguments in writing, and as Tom Percy said at the start of his oral submission, " ... the written submissions and the note from before that ... relieves me of the obligation to go through exhaustively a number of the matters that we've set out there ..." DPP Coates , on the other hand, seemed to have no compunction to go through his submission "exhaustively".

The key issue, the major item of fresh and compelling evidence presented by Percy was to do with the DNA analysis. Given that DNA is one of the most powerful tools of evidence in criminal investigations and trials, it seems extraordinary that the investigators and the DPP had always played down its importance, ever since the matching of the DNA sample from *Four Winds* with that of Meaghan Vass in March 2010, six months before the trial. The then DPP, prosecutor Tim Ellis SC called it a 'big red herring', to the extent of denying it was relevant in Sue Neill-Fraser's request for leave to appeal to the High Court back in 2011, thus steering the High Court away from considering the case.

An informed observer could be forgiven for concluding that the prosecution did not WANT to discover evidence that in any way undermined its case against Sue Neill-Fraser. That, of course, would have been highly improper, unethical and against the law.

Now, finally, the DNA issue was coming to a head. And with the evidence from the most recent expert witness in these hearings, Max Jones (report July 2014, Victoria Police Forensic Service), Percy had the ammunition to make it the leading item of fresh evidence. Jones had said the DNA sample was most likely to be a direct transfer, in complete reversal of the view that had been left with the jury at trial, where it had been played down as being secondary transfer, of no import.

In response, Coates suggested that defence counsel for Sue, the late David Gunson SC, could have got this evidence with reasonable diligence. I wondered if Coates realised the full import of what he was saying? He was effectively undermining the reliability of the Tasmanian Forensic Science Service, on which the prosecution relied for the evidence about the DNA sample. He was implying that the defence perhaps should have had another service perform a test to check the prosecution's own evidence. That suggestion is contrary to the rules: the defence is entitled to accept the Crown's evidence as reliable.

Percy quoted the relevant precedent from Justice Peek's decision in the successful 2015 appeal under South Australia's (similar) new legislation by the convicted Adrian Drummond:

> *"One must take into account that counsel is entitled to assume that the prosecution will disclose to the defence in relevant evidence and material in a fortiori that the prosecution will not lead false or misleading evidence as part of its case."*

A number of further grounds were cited by Percy, before Coates got to his feet for his closing marathon ... to be continued a week later.

Combined with the objections detailed by the DPP, Coates, the delay seemed yet another way to frustrate the attempt to enquire into Neill-Fraser's conviction. Every effort was being made, it seemed, to ensure that the trial would avoid new scrutiny. The Crown was eager to discount the relevance of the large sample of Meaghan Vass' DNA, to urge on the court that it was merely a sample of secondary transfer, perhaps on the shoe of a policeman. It would have been a physically freaky cop to have had shoes to transport a large amount of DNA-bearing bodily fluids on the deck of *Four Winds,* in a swabbed area of 210 mm x 260 mm, the size of a pancake, as measured by Forensic Science Services Tasmania (on January 30, 2009), 9.45 metres from the forward end of Four Winds and 250 mm from the starboard rail. Not to mention the absence of any other shoe-borne sample on the deck.

This was part of the testimony at the trial on September 29, 2010 of D. McHoul of the Tasmanian Forensic Science Service about the swab that tested positive to DNA. From this moment on, the court, the prosecution and defence all knew that the deposit from which the DNA sample was taken was 210 x 260 mm in size. But the jury, while aware of it, were never reminded of it at the critical time/s by defence counsel, to challenge the transfer suggestion.

There was initially no match with the DNA - until March 2010, when it was matched with then homeless 15 year old Hobart girl, Meaghan Vass. Neill-Fraser had already been arrested and was on remand awaiting trial. In her short appearance in the witness box at trial, Vass simply denied she had been on board and the prosecution carried on with its case.

At the August 2011 appeal, the DPP told the court (CT p66):

> *the expert said 'a large amount of DNA' that was confused with 'a large stain or a large amount of fluid'. That wasn't the case at all. It was simply a case of a strong result from a swab. So how large the stain was we don't know."*

That was not correct; the DPP did know how large the stain was and had known since September 29, 2010 - a year earlier.

The DPP continued:

> *The expert told the Court that the DNA could have got there in a multitude of ways, it could have been attached to the shoe of someone who subsequently walked on the boat, it could have been perhaps from Ms Vass spitting in the vicinity of the boat while it was tied up at Constitution Dock or Goodwood. But there is absolutely no basis to have suggested that its presence linked her, in a way that any sensible jury would take notice of, to the murder."*

Not as a suspect, sure, but very likely she would have made a valuable eye witness - for the defence, as it turned out.

On 7 September, 2012, two years after the trial, there was an application for special leave to appeal to the High Court. The appeal concerned the test that the court used to not allow the recall of the homeless girl Vass after she had given evidence and it became apparent from the evidence from a police officer (that had not been previously disclosed to the Defence) that Vass had lied to personnel at Mara House about her movements on the night and given a false address – evidence which was later ruled to be inadmissible.

Defence counsel argued that the finding of the DNA was a very important and powerful consideration because it pointed to a hypothesis consistent with Sue's innocence. There was discussion about the potential significance of her evidence with the DPP arguing that there was "*nothing else to connect her [Vass] or make her a remotely possible suspect except for the presence of a swab of DNA*" (at page 11).

Moreover, the DPP argued at page 12:

> *The core evidence was … she was not on the boat. She had no way of being on the boat. There was nothing credible suggested as to how she could be on the boat.*

And the DPP again at page 13:

> *There is just no other connection besides DNA, one piece of DNA; no fingerprints, nothing else, and a piece of DNA found in a common walkway, not in relation to the real scene of the crime which was below decks*

Further, the DPP at page 13:

> *… a very strong case where all the circumstances pointed to the applicant and to the applicant only. They did not point to a homeless 15-year old girl. (emphasis added)*

The High Court accepted those points and refused leave to appeal. It could be argued they were not properly informed, denied the information about the deposit.

To this day, we mused around the kitchen table, the police and the Crown still insist that this DNA sample is a 'big red herring' as then prosecutor Tim Ellis told the jury. Sarah has been exemplary in keeping calm. She made another coffee and I marvelled at her composure.

On Oct 31, 2017, Coates had cross examined Max Jones of the Victorian Police Forensic Service and attempted to elicit an answer that would deny the DNA being a direct transfer:

> *And is it fair to say that you don't rule out the possibility that that sample got there via a secondary transfer?......I can't entirely rule that possibility out. Although I will stipulate that it would require a specific set of circumstances that – perhaps ideal conditions for that transfer to occur to that extent to produce such a good DNA profile from this sample.*

Indeed: the sample was so strong it had to be diluted tenfold so as not to present as overamplified, suggesting its origins as possibly saliva or phlegm. That is not typical of the 'touch scenario' or secondary transfer.

Coates avoided - as the Crown and the police had done throughout the history of the case - considering any line of enquiry and any evidence that did not support the tunnel vision proposition that Neill-Fraser was guilty. For the Crown to resist an appeal (with even earlier efforts to delay or frustrate the process) in the face of the extensive disquiet expressed in public by respected QCs, other lawyers and interested observers, invited the consideration that the conviction would not stand such scrutiny. Why else?

Flying back to Sydney on August 24, 2018, after that latest adjournment, I asked 'why' myself, thinking that not only does Tasmania's legal system stand to lose the confidence of the public, the Crown's resistance to a further review of the case in the appeal court suggests to me there is less concern for seeking justice than justification.

That view was reinforced while awaiting further developments - that is, the judgement of Justice Brett as to whether to grant leave to appeal.

Just one last item to be cleared up: Meaghan Vass and her 'yes I was / no I wasn't on the yacht' affidavits, the latest of which the prosecution said was not only coerced from her, but was the work of McLaren as an "unlicenced private investigator" (Max. penalty $31,800), an allegation by the DPP.

At the December 11, 2018, directions hearing, Remy van de Weil KC, appearing on behalf of author Colin McLaren, advised Justice Brett of McLaren's serious heart condition and that while McLaren was keen to assist, the undue stress of travelling to and appearing in the Hobart court might be too stressful. McLaren could provide his evidence by video link. Van de Weil KC went on to advise the judge that the Prosecutor and junior, Jack Shapiro, were wrongly referring to McLaren as an unlicenced private investigator, explaining to the court that he worked as an author (6 books, working on his 7th) and documentary film-maker (20 projects) and was hired by film producer Eve Ash, in the role of writer/author and consultant to her production.

This to me was evidence of panic within the Office of the DPP. McLaren had, after all, accompanied by Eve Ash, hand delivered a dossier of over 50 pages to Tasmanian authorities with the results of his investigation, back in the first half of 2017. He was certainly not employed by Neill-Fraser's legal team to 'gather evidence to be used in court proceedings' as if had been acting as a private investigator. It's just that he showed 'em up at TasPol.

The media dam broke on Australia Day 2019, the 10th anniversary of Bob Chappell's disappearance from the *Four Winds*. On that day, it was my blog, *wrongfulconvictionsreport.org* that published what triggered a torrent of stories on the case. Two days later, Colin McLaren's book, *Southern Justice* (Hachette) was launched, with plenty of media coverage - including a series of articles on *wrongfulconvictionsreport.org* over the following two weeks. Three days after that, on January 30, Channel 7 broadcast (except in Tasmania) the first of 6 x 1 hour TV documentaries, *Undercurrent,* a deep dive investigation into the case by filmmaker Eve Ash (*Shadow of Doubt*, 2013) and CJZ Productions; McLaren was involved as investigative reporter. This bombshell series revealed all the flaws of the police investigation, all the evidence and all witnesses that were missed, and more. It certainly shook the public's confidence in the conviction.

The next hearing in the Supreme Court on February 5, 2019, generated more media coverage, and two weeks later, on February 19, the third book investigating the Neill-Fraser case came out: Robin Bowles' *Death on the Derwent* (Scribe), generating yet more media. It, too, detailed how the conviction was wrong.

On the heels of *Undercurrent*, Channel 9's *60 Minutes* on Sunday, March 10, 2019, ran a three-segment long interview with Meaghan Vass, in which she for the first time in public, specifically admitted that she had witnessed the bloody fight (perhaps the murder or manslaughter). She was there, as her DNA on the deck suggested. It was a highly emotional and credible public confession that confirms her as an eye witness, nothwithstanding the Crown's dismissal of her testimony.

This interview energised the national interest - and fired up Neill-Fraser's many loyal supporters.

THE 60 MINUTES TRANSCRIPT

Journalist Liam Bartlett interviews Meaghan Vass and narrates the story, interspersed with other interviews – Robert Richter KC, Sarah Bowles, Colin McLaren – and documentary footage and recreation. Only the Vass interview clips are transcribed below.

.... Liam Bartlett introduces the story.

LIAM BARTLETT: So, you know who killed Bob Chappell?
MEAGHAN VASS: (*Nods, anguished*) Ah, yes.
LIAM BARTLETT: And it certainly wasn't Sue Neill-Fraser?
MEAGHAN VASS: No.

.... Liam Bartlett introduces further information.

LIAM BARTLETT: If what you're saying is true, then...
MEAGHAN VASS: I've no reason to lie. (*Inhales, anguished*)
LIAM BARTLETT: Then Sue Neill-Fraser has been in jail for nothing. What do you think about that?
MEAGHAN VASS: I think it's horrible but...

.... Liam Bartlett explains the DNA evidence, interviews Robert Richter KC re Meaghan's latest account now fitting with the objective evidence.

LIAM BARTLETT: Why should we believe you, now? Give me one good reason.
MEAGHAN VASS: I don't, I don't have a good reason, really, but... I'm hoping you do but I've realised it's the right thing to do and I'd like to see her home with her family. (*Inhales deeply, eyes closed, holds her throat.*)

.... Liam Bartlett explains background to Bob Chappell missing, boat sinking, and Sue Neill-Fraser's arrest, interview Sarah Bowles, interview with Robert Richter KC re the forensic disaster, and the ignoring of the DNA evidence.

LIAM BARTLETT: Tell me a bit about what life was like for you in Hobart, you know, around that time.
MEAGHAN VASS: Hard, I was living in women's shelters, and on the streets. It's pretty hard.
LIAM BARTLETT: Very hard. What, why was that? Did you have problems at home?
MEAGHAN VASS: Um, yeah. Family relationship breakdown, (*clears throat*) – at thirteen – um and that resulted in women's shelters and...
LIAM BARTLETT: That's very difficult, isn't it, for such a young girl too.
MEAGHAN VASS: Yeah it's been really massive.

.... Liam Bartlett explains Meaghan's background.

LIAM BARTLETT: Why's it taken you this long to speak up?
MEAGHAN VASS: (*Anguished*) I don't know. I've had, I've lost my father, I've been living on the streets, (*crying*) I've been hounded by everybody. It's the right thing to do. Please. (*Reaches for more tissues*)
LIAM BARTLETT: What, what sort of things have you had to put up with?
MEAGHAN VASS: (*teary, upset*) Well I've had no shelter, I've had no safety. I've had no, you know, I haven't been able to fend for myself, properly. I've had no one to turn to. (*Gasps*)

LIAM BARTLETT: Do you trust the police?
MEAGHAN VASS: No, not really. (*Sniffs, wipes tears from her face.*)

.... Liam Bartlett talks of Meaghan's drug usage.

LIAM BARTLETT: Are you clean now?
MEAGHAN VASS: Yes, yes. (*wipes tears from her face*).
LIAM BARTLETT: How long have you been clean?
MEAGHAN VASS: Oh, it's, it's only recent. Ah yeah, it's been hard (*grimaces*). It's been hard *(whispers*).
LIAM BARTLETT: Are you still trying to stay off it?
MEAGHAN VASS: (*nodding*)
LIAM BARTLETT: It's a struggle, isn't it? I can see that.
MEAGHAN VASS: (*Distraught, silently nods, holds back tears*)
LIAM BARTLETT: I can see that.
MEAGHAN VASS: (*Winces, almost breaking*)
LIAM BARTLETT: Do you think this will – this will help you?
MEAGHAN VASS: (*Nods*)
LIAM BARTLETT: Telling the truth will help you?
MEAGHAN VASS: Yes, I'm...
LIAM BARTLETT: Will help you with that struggle?
MEAGHAN VASS: I'm hoping, anyway. (*Sniffs, braces*)

.... Liam Bartlett narrates re Meaghan's version differing to police version.

LIAM BARTLETT: So, on that day, why did you decide to go out into the bay?
MEAGHAN VASS: I would have been (*clears throat*) along with

him, I reckon, um and no doubt he would have been knocking things off boats, um for money to get on, get on the piss and that being the case, I would have, you know, gone along, gone along with that but, not so that I would so much steal, but y'know to have a drink, or…

LIAM BARTLETT: Yeah, you were just tagging along?

MEAGHAN VASS: Yeah. Yep. It was something that they'd – he'd do often.

…. Liam Bartlett explains how they met up with an older homeless man.

LIAM BARTLETT: If they knew Bob Chappell was on board, would they have…

MEAGHAN VASS: Probably not.

LIAM BARTLETT: Got on that yacht?

MEAGHAN VASS: I mean, I can't answer for them, I suppose but … probably not.

…. Liam Bartlett describes Meaghan being haunted.

MEAGHAN VASS: I can remember being on board. And person that I was with, (*breathes deeply*) obviously been spotted by Bob, I don't know. Been told to piss off, they've had an argument, it's escalated, he's hit Bob, I don't know what with -

LIAM BARTLETT: So he struck him?

MEAGHAN VASS: Quite a few times I think. Probably twenty minutes or so, I… (*holds her throat*)

LIAM BARTLETT: Twenty minutes?

MEAGHAN VASS: Roundabouts. I'm, I…

LIAM BARTLETT: It went on for a while?

MEAGHAN VASS: Yeah (*still holding throat, looking away, anguished*). And then I, I saw, I saw a lot of blood, but I can't, sorry, I can't give you any more than that, I can't remember. (*Breathes deeply, looks down, shakes her head*)
LIAM BARTLETT: The guy you were with, was hitting Bob Chappell?
MEAGHAN VASS: (*Wipes face, nods*)
LIAM BARTLETT: Can you remember what he was hitting him with?
MEAGHAN VASS: No. (*Holds throat*)
LIAM BARTLETT: And, and did you try to break it up?
MEAGHAN VASS: I, I would have told, (*clears throat*) would have told the bloke I was seeing to stop or to calm down, but there's, (*sighs deeply*) there's only so much I could do. I'm only small and he's a bigger bloke. And so I couldn't get him to calm down, you know -
LIAM BARTLETT: When you say there was a lot of blood, were you downstairs, were you on the deck, were you in the cabin or?
MEAGHAN VASS: I can't (*shakes head, hand on throat*) – on the deck I think.
LIAM BARTLETT: And what was your reaction to that?
MEAGHAN VASS: It's when I've thrown up, the vomit. (*Rests chin on hand*)

.... Liam Bartlett describes the reason for Meaghan vomiting on the deck.

LIAM BARTLETT: So what mistake did Bob make? What did Bob do wrong? MEAGHAN VASS: Nothing – oh (*shreds tissues apart*).

LIAM BARTLETT: Nothing at all?

MEAGHAN VASS: Well he just told (*NAME BEEPED*) to piss off I spose. (*Sniffs*)

LIAM BARTLETT: He was just at the wrong place, wrong time?

MEAGHAN VASS: (*Nods*) Yes please are we nearly done? (*Whispers*)

LIAM BARTLETT: Do you know what happened to Bob's body?

MEAGHAN VASS: No. (*Holds throat, shakes head*) Not saying, but whatever's happened it's been horrible.

LIAM BARTLETT: What, what was the second man doing?

MEAGHAN VASS: Oh, I gather that the bloke that I was with just called him down to the cabin.

LIAM BARTLETT: Did you go back to shore, while they were dealing with that or did you stay on the boat?

MEAGHAN VASS: I must have gone back to shore but I can't, I can't recollect how.

LIAM BARTLETT: But, but you know that Bob Chappell was killed by one of the men you were with? Is that what you're telling me?

MEAGHAN VASS: Yeh.

LIAM BARTLETT: Are you certain about that?

MEAGHAN VASS: Yes.

LIAM BARTLETT: Did you see Sue Neill-Fraser on that yacht?

MEAGHAN VASS: No.

LIAM BARTLETT: She wasn't there?

MEAGHAN VASS: Not that I can recall, no.

LIAM BARTLETT: But if what you're saying is true, then an innocent woman has been sitting in jail for nine years.

MEAGHAN VASS: (*Wipes nose, sniffs*) Yes.

.... Liam Bartlett describes Meaghan's courage to speak, and believing her, Sue should be free.

MEAGHAN VASS: We'd been on board and the person that I was with, (*breathes deeply*) obviously been spotted by Bob. I don't know, been told to piss off, they've had an argument, it's escalated, he's hit Bob I don't know what with, and then I, I (*holding throat*) saw, saw a lot of blood, but I can't, sorry I can't give you any more than that, I can't remember.
.... Liam Bartlett describes Meaghan's shock, vomiting on deck, fear of telling truth and now killer is walking free.

LIAM BARTLETT: What's that man doing now?
MEAGHAN VASS: Um, not a real lot, I don't think.
LIAM BARTLETT: And how angry is he going to be at you for telling the truth? MEAGHAN VASS: Probably furious. But.. (*shrugs*) I'd just like, I'd just like to see her get home to her family.
LIAM BARTLETT: But why now, after ten years?
MEAGHAN VASS: Because it's the right thing to do, it'd, you know?
LIAM BARTLETT: But you, you could have done it eight years ago, nine years ago. You could have done it at the trial.
MEAGHAN VASS: Can I stop please, now? (*frustrated, moves her hair*)
LIAM BARTLETT: Well, you can, but I just want you now to tell me from your heart.
MEAGHAN VASS: I've told you I have no, I don't have a legit, a legitimate reason for you but I'm saying that, you know, I'm here and now, I like her to go home. I'd like to see her home with her family.

.... Colin McLaren interview re Meaghan's fear, forensics and missing key exhibits, evidence ignored, Vass' boyfriend ignored, Liam Bartlett narrates.

.... Liam Bartlett narrates intro to next section, re Meaghan's previous denials about being on the yacht.

LIAM BARTLETT: The trial of Sue Neill-Fraser, you were sixteen, at the time.

MEAGHAN VASS: Yes.

LIAM BARTLETT: Why, why didn't you tell the truth?

MEAGHAN VASS: Because, I was sixteen, I was homeless, I was scared, I, you know, huh, it's huge, it's been daunting.

LIAM BARTLETT: What were you scared of?

MEAGHAN VASS: I was scared of everything, I...

LIAM BARTLETT: Tell me, explain that to me.

MEAGHAN VASS: Well, what if, you know, his reaction maybe?

LIAM BARTLETT: Who? The man who killed Bob?

MEAGHAN VASS: Yeah.

LIAM BARTLETT: Did he tell you to shut up?

MEAGHAN VASS: Yes, now can I stop please?

.... Liam Bartlett explains Meaghan's silence till her 2017 statement saying she was there with two unnamed males, but then retracting it.

LIAM BARTLETT: Why did you change your mind then?

MEAGHAN VASS: I don't know (*shakes her head*).

LIAM BARTLETT: Did anybody put pressure on you?

MEAGHAN VASS: (*Shakes her head*) Just fear of it all, I think.

LIAM BARTLETT: Why have you let her sit in a jail cell for all these years? MEAGHAN VASS: I haven't been asked, I haven't been able to recall all of this. Agh.

LIAM BARTLETT: Haven't been able to or haven't wanted to?

MEAGHAN VASS: Probably haven't wanted to, I don't.

LIAM BARTLETT: So why do you want, why do you want to set the record straight now?

MEAGHAN VASS: Because it's the right thing to do, I s'pose, I don't know *(whispered, distraught).*

LIAM BARTLETT: So, you know who killed Bob Chappell?

MEAGHAN VASS: (*Nods, anguished*) Ah, yes.

LIAM BARTLETT: And it certainly wasn't Sue Neill-Fraser?

MEAGHAN VASS: No.

LIAM BARTLETT: What would you like to see happen to Sue Neill-Fraser?

MEAGHAN VASS: I'd like her to be able to go home to her family. I don't have one, you know... (*gasps*) so, sorry ... (*distraught)*

LIAM BARTLETT: That's okay.

MEAGHAN VASS: That's what I'd like and *(head shaking*).

LIAM BARTLETT: You know the names of the two men who were involved in this murder. What do you intend to do with that information?

MEAGHAN VASS: (*wiping eyes*) I don't want, I'm not confident um saying a name. yeah.

LIAM BARTLETT: But are you prepared to give those names to the police? MEAGHAN VASS: No ... no, this is as far as I ...

.... Liam Bartlett narrates, re Meaghan's new affidavit naming the men, interview with Robert Richter KC who says must have Royal Commission.

LIAM BARTLETT: Sooner or later for Sue Neill-Fraser to be released, you'll have to go back to a courtroom.
MEAGHAN VASS: Yeah.
LIAM BARTLETT: Will you be able to handle that?
MEAGHAN VASS: (*Nods, wipes nose*)
LIAM BARTLETT: You won't go back on your story again?
MEAGHAN VASS: No.
LIAM BARTLETT: How, how can you be so sure, this time round?
MEAGHAN VASS: I just, I just am.

.... Liam Bartlett explains how Meaghan giving up her secret should help Sue Neill-Fraser to be released.

MEAGHAN VASS: I can't give a legitimate reason as to why anyone should believe me. And given my track record, yeah maybe they shouldn't. But I'm here now and I'm doing all I can. I can't, I can't do any more than that.
LIAM BARTLETT: Do you feel guilty for allowing an innocent woman to remain in jail?
MEAGHAN VASS: Yeah it's been pretty horrible, yeah (*grimaces, braces*).
LIAM BARTLETT: So the day Sue Neill-Fraser is released, for something she didn't do, will that be a happy day for you?
MEAGHAN VASS: (*Nods, anguished*)
LIAM BARTLETT: What would you like to say to her?
MEAGHAN VASS: Dunno ... sorry for it all really. Mm, just hope she can go home to her family (*sniffs*).
LIAM BARTLETT: You're sorry.
MEAGHAN VASS: (*Nods, anguished*)

LIAM BARTLETT: For not speaking up.
MEAGHAN VASS: (*Nods, anguished*)

(Transcript courtesy Eve Ash)

All this activity was like an express train speeding towards the end of the line in the extended process of seeking leave to appeal. Justice Brett asked for the affidavit from Vass that would confirm her admission as sworn testimony in the process. It was to be delivered on March 21. Just over 24 hours prior to the 4pm hearing on that day, the news spread through the social networks that Justice Brett would actually deliver his decision at that time. And he did - he granted leave to appeal, at around 5pm on March 21, 2019, in the following terms:

> 48. After reserving my decision in this application, the applicant applied to reopen her case for the purpose of presentation of some further evidence. I was told from the bar table, without objection, that the evidence relates to an interview conducted with Ms Vass by a journalist during the course of a 60 Minutes program that was aired on television recently. I was aware from media advertisements for the program that the interview was to be aired, but this did not occur in Tasmania and I have not seen the interview. There was no objection by the respondent to the reopening of the application or to the presentation of the evidence.
> 49. The evidence provided to me consists of an affidavit by Ms Vass. The affidavit purports to have been sworn

on 25 February 2019. The affidavit contains direct and detailed admissions of Ms Vass's involvement in events aboard the Four Winds on the relevant night. In particular, Ms Vass states that she was present on the yacht then with two identified male companions. She witnessed at least one of the males assault Mr Chappell. She recalls seeing a lot of blood. The affidavit does not directly address what became of Mr Chappell. Ms Vass claims that she cannot recall leaving the yacht or what happened after the assault.

54. In this case, I am satisfied that the applicant has a reasonable case to present to the Court in support of the ground of appeal, and that it is in the interests of justice for leave to be granted. The fresh and compelling evidence to which this decision refers is the evidence of the out of court representations of Ms Vass. Insofar as it has been submitted that the evidence is not reliable, I am satisfied that it would be reasonably open to the Court of Criminal Appeal to accept such evidence as credible and providing a trustworthy basis for fact finding. I reiterate that I am not making a positive determination to that effect. However, I am satisfied that there is nothing about this evidence that would enable me to form a positive conclusion that the Court of Criminal Appeal would necessarily reject the evidence as unreliable.

And with that, the next chapter in the saga of Sue Neill-Fraser's tumultuous journey through Tasmania's legal system began.

Actually, it had begun with the police reaction to the *60 Minutes* interview with Vass. On March 7, police picked her up at a bus stop, searched her bag and tried to get her to talk about her admission of being on the yacht and witnessing the murder, that was going to be aired on *60 Minutes,* as promos for the program revealed. The day after the program went to air - except in Tasmania - the police issued a statement: *Assistant Commissioner Richard Cowling said police re-interviewed Ms Vass last week when the program's promotional material suggested a new version of events.*

The version of events given by Ms Vass on 60 Minutes is contrary to her previous police interview, contrary to her sworn evidence in court and ***contrary to last week's police interview,*** *" Commander Cowling said. (emphasis added).*

But as fate would have it, or karma if you prefer, police charging Vass with minor marijuana possession charges when they 're-interviewed' her, turned out to be an opportunity for Vass to rebut the claim that she had said anything "contrary" to her 60 Minutes interview.

At her court appearance on April 18, the prosecution told Deputy Chief Magistrate Daly that Vass had said 'No comment' to everything put to her by police when she was picked up for questioning on Thursday March 7. That directly contradicts what Commander Cowling had stated.

The facts presented to court also correct the false impression created by the unsourced story in *The Australian* published on Monday, April 14, 2019, by Matthew Denholm, headlined *Yacht murder witness changes her tune again,* that Vass had recanted to police in the previous few days. I published Vass' denial of that on Tuesday, April 16, in a story that corresponds with the facts stated in court by the prosecution on Thursday, April 18.

When I rang Denholm to check just who was his source for the story, he wouldn't say; but he said he was confident of his facts. The Hobart Mercury on April 16 repeated Denholm's story, qualified as "reportedly".

The problem here, of course, is twofold: 1) it appears to be misleading, which would be seriously unlawful and 2) it is prejudicial to Vass and thus to Neill-Fraser. In the event her appeal is successful, there could well be a retrial - with a jury. A jury whose collective mind has been poisoned by this information about the key witness.

I wrote to Attorney-General Elise Archer on April 23, 2018, to draw her attention to the matter, but she claimed to be unable to comment or act as the case was before the courts. That did not seem to have bothered Commander Cowling.

I also wrote to Attorney-General Elise Archer on a couple of occasions to enquire (unsuccessfully) if and when she might establish a review into the case. On March 24, 2022, I again wrote to her, saying: "It has been a month now since I requested your response to the Etter Selby papers concerning the Sue Neill-Fraser case that were tabled in Parliament on August 31, 2021.

"I also provided legal advice (obtained from Dr Bob Moles) that clearly shows "the case has not been before the courts since her appeal was dismissed last year; the High Court has not been engaged as her application has not been accepted to date. In other words, you are legally free to comment on the matter.

"I have come to the disappointing conclusion that you are not only ignoring my request for comment but you are also ignoring the contents of the Etter Selby dossier.

"This correspondence will serve at any future review or enquiry as a record of your consistent refusal to engage with the legally supported evidence that questions the Neill-Fraser conviction."

* The author's trips to Hobart for Court hearings seeking leave to appeal: Oct 29 - Nov 3, 2017 / Feb 22 - 25, 2018 / March 6 - 10, 2018 / June 25 - 30, 2018 / Aug 19 - 24, 2018 / Feb 5 - 6, 2019

THE BLEAK HISTORY OF CALLS FOR AN INQUIRY/REVIEW

Formal, reasoned letters from barristers requesting a review of the Sue Neill-Fraser case, reports identifying errors warranting a review or a Royal Commission, public rallies, a substantial, well documented dossier revealing failings of the police investigation - and a petition with over 36,000 signatures (as at early 2023) … have all been effectively ignored by Tasmania's political leadership or simply stated 'every confidence' in the state's legal system.

August 2, 2013 letter to A-G Brian Wightman
From Robert Richter KC & Greg Barns SC
IGNORED

August 2013 Tasmanian Parliament
From Dr Bob Moles, for independent review
IGNORED

May 2017 Premier, Acting A-G, Solicitor General
Disclosures in White Paper from research for Undercurrent documentary
Eve Ash, Colin McClaren, Robert Richter KC
IGNORED

September 13, 2018
Former Premier Lara Giddings, for a Criminal Cases Review Commission (Ref Neill-Fraser)
IGNORED

January 28, 2019 to A-G Elise Archer
From Civil Liberties Australia, proposal for a Royal Commission / Commission of Inquiry
DISMISSED

August 20, 2019
From Robert Richter KC & filmmaker Eve Ash for Royal Commission
IGNORED

August 2021 – February 24, 2022 to A-G Elise Archer
The Etter/Selby papers
IGNORED

October 2021 to Members of Tasmanian Parliament
Report by Dr Bob Moles and Bibi Sangha
IGNORED

December 18, 2021 public rally
Andrew Wilkie MP, calling for independent review
IGNORED

January 2022 to A-G Elise Archer
From Tony Jacobs, former prosecutor, proposal for Enquiry Panel
IGNORED

November 2022 to A-G Elise Archer
From Robert Richter KC & David Edwardson
IGNORED

May 2023 to A-G Elise Archer
From Tony Jacobs, former prosecutor
REBUFFED*

PETITION urging a review signed by 36,000 + (still active)
IGNORED

*The Attorney-General replied with her template response as detailed in The Road to Exoneration.

THE MISSED CLUES IN SUE NEILL-FRASER'S STATUTORY DECLARATION

At 12.10pm on Friday, February 28, 2009, just a day after her partner Bob Chappell had been found missing from their yacht, *Four Winds*, Sue Neill-Fraser began making a Statutory Declaration at her Allison Street home in front of Detective Sergeant Simon Conroy of TasPol. The shock of it all - her loving partner of 18 years had disappeared, perhaps ... probably ... hurt, their new dream yacht was damaged and sinking, ... her world suddenly empty and uncertain. But she had always been undemonstrative, calm and reserved. There was no hysteria or weeping. Maybe there should have been.

The stat dec was standard procedure. She had not requested to be accompanied by a lawyer. She had no concerns that she would need a lawyer. No one had then thought Chappell had been murdered. No one imagined Neill-Fraser was a murderer. Her demeanour, her previous small business with her horses and her middle class circle of friends all spoke silently of a woman who never stepped out of line.

That Stat Dec was presented at her trial on October 1, 2010. It should never have got to the court; the statement contains enough raw information to establish to TasPol that strangers had been aboard the yacht. The TasPol missed it completely. Or ignored it. Or was it all too hard? Too embarrassing?

My full name is Susan Blyth Neill-Fraser. This is the second statement I have made regarding the disappearance of my partner, Robert Adrian Chappell. This statement is regarding my observations from viewing my vessel, the Four Winds, last evening. At the request of police I attended the vessel, which was moored at Constitution Dock 27/1/09. I noticed a number of things which were not as I knew them to have been left or that were in my opinion highly unusual.

These are – At the back of the boat it appeared to be the gate had been lifted off and pulled back quickly with the bottom latch out of its seat. Having been on the boat in heavy weather and the gate not moving this had to have been purposely moved in my opinion.

At the entrance to the wheelhouse there was new damage to the running board which supports the sliding hatch or the framework around the hatch. The damage appeared to be from a rope being under load and running over the timber work. The green self pearling sheet (rope) should have been tied up in storage at the back of the boat instead it was tied around the winch on the rear mast and had been cut. Secondly, the green main mast boom sheet (rope) should have been in a rope bag to the right of the cabin entrance instead it was on the deck and appeared to have been threaded off the winch. From the damage to the timber work it appeared that this was the cause –

The next points noticed were at the main mast. A black sheet (rope) was out of place. It should have been in a locker at the back left of the boat which was attached to a cleat at the mast, the rope had been freshly cut and a substantial length of it is missing. Secondly, at this point there is a red sheet slightly thinner than the black it had also been cut. It was attached to the smaller winch at the front of the mast; in place was a winch handle. This winch handle should have been stored either in a basket on the rear wall of the wheelhouse or in the locker at the rear of the vessel.

Observations from within the vessel are as follows –

As you enter the wheelhouse on the right we had mounted a new EPIRB, it is a 406 and registered to our vessel, the EPIRB was mounted by Bob. He knew how to properly remove it from its bracket. The release tab was broken from the bracket. To do this the EPIRB must have been forcefully pulled away from the bracket –

Next moving into the saloon I immediately noticed that the flooring was missing. This would not have floated free when the vessel flooded, it had to have many screws taken out to lift it up. Bob knew that this was a difficult job and had no reason to remove the floor. I'm sure he would not have removed the flooring. In the hole left were two screwdrivers, these were from our toolkit. The floor is covered by carpeted pieces. There were around eight square pieces of carpet which were square pieces. The spare pieces were possibly stored in the laundry. Just before the laundry door was a mounted fire extinguisher. This fire extinguisher was an older style, it was bracketed in place and I think out of commission. Rather than worry about it we simply purchased newer and lighter extinguishers for the vessel. This particular extinguisher was very heavy. It was secured in place and again had survived rough seas on our journey from Queensland so I knew it – so I know it hasn't come loose in the flood – there was obvious damage to the pipe leading from the seacock to the toilet. This pipe had been cut through – from the galley I cannot locate two knives, a Wiltshire knife is missing, this would have had a round with a six to seven inch blade. It was originally mine, have had it a long time. Another similar knife is also missing. I remember when I went to the boat on Monday we ate some fruit cake. I used one of these knives to cut the cake. I can't exactly recall if I passed the knife through to the wheelhouse from the galley and cut the cake there or if I sliced the cake in the galley. I will recognize this knife again, they came with the boat – I believe a fire extinguisher may be missing, I'm sure there were three on board but I only think I saw two when I was looking last night – regarding the electrical circuitry we were paranoid about the boat being damaged or sinking, we always checked the circuit boards to make sure that the switches were correctly positioned.

The circuit breakers for the bilge pumps were always to be positioned in the on position and bilges on automatic. If the circuit breakers were off the bilges would not work. Bob would absolutely not turn off the circuit breakers for the bilges off. I cannot think of any circumstance where he would turn them off. When I left Bob on the vessel I took the tender dinghy, this was usual practice. Bob did not like to have to get in and out of the dinghy unless totally necessary. It was usual practice for me to take the dinghy. It was simply Bob's preference that this is the way it was done. Bob was not terribly nimble about the boat or the tender dinghy, it was actually safer for me to take the dinghy than for him to operate it by himself and try to get aboard the bigger boat. The actual location I tied the tender to was outside the Royal Hobart Yacht Club. It was near a steel ladder from the dock in the area where the Royal have their small club yachts on moorings. I am now sure I secured the dinghy properly with three knots.

Bob and my financial arrangements were largely separate. We often transferred money between bank accounts. As Bob was the primary income earner he would transfer five hundred dollars per fortnight to me for our living expenses. Costs for the boat we split fifty fifty. Sometimes one paid in full and the other reimbursed. The EPIRB on the boat came with the boat, it was new and still in the box when we picked it up. Bob mounted it. I registered it last week with AMSA via the internet.

Further thought has been given to my timings on the 26/1/09. We firstly went to the yacht in the morning about 9:00am. We had a cup of tea and cake for morning tea. This was around 10:00am to 10:30am. I returned home at about 11:00am to 11:30 and had a shower. Time from then on is difficult as my mobile phone is the only source of time and I left it with Bob. Anne, Bob's sister and I went to the Royal Hobart Yacht Club for lunch. Lunch was not being served so we had a drink and a pie there. We then took photos on the dock. I then drove Anne home at around 1:00. I then returned to Marieville Esplanade. The wind was getting up and I thought I'd better get to the boat and see if Bob wanted to leave the boat. When I got to the tender the outboard was buried and I needed help getting it free. This was near the rowing club, a different position from the Royal where I later tied it. The wind was up and the chop got me very wet. I tied the tender up to the side of the boat, the leeward side, which was the right hand side. I did not stay onboard very long. Bob was a bit snappy. I was of the opinion Bob could have come off the boat due to the weather. Bob had checked the chart and said the wind would drop out and said he had decided to stay on the boat. In the end I left him the mobile. I asked if I should pick him in the morning for work. He said he may not even go to work. So I left it at that and thought he would ring me if he wanted. I was sure he would change his mind later and call me to get him.

Given the wind, I decided not to take the tender to Marieville Esplanade, I decided to take it to the Royal Yacht Club where it would be easily managed. From tying it up I went to Bunnings Hardware on the Brooker then came home. Anne was not home by then, as it was getting late. Anne had gone to Bruny Island for the night. She was being picked up after 4 pm I am sure when I got home it was starting to get dark. I stayed out at Bunnings for a long time. I did not buy anything but browsed. I drove our Ford Falcon Station wagon. I stayed alone at home that night. I made several phone calls and received a call from Richard King over some family matters. It was ten thirty pm when I got off the phone. The following morning I was notified that the Four Winds was sinking by the police radio room. I then went to Sandy Bay.

Sue Neill-Fraser made this statement the day after the *Four Winds* was found to be slowly taking water, Bob Chappell missing. Clues should have been obvious in her then fresh statement, which could have helped the police investigation, which at that stage might have been listed under Missing Persons.

1. Neill-Fraser's description of damage to the boat - the rear gate lifted off, new damage to the running board, disarranged and cut ropes, damage to the timber work, EPIRB release tab broken and the unit forcibly pulled from the bracket, missing flooring, cut pipes, missing knives, bilge pump circuit breakers disarmed - is a clear, multi-pronged clue that stranger/s had caused the damage.
2. The apparent violence that caused some of the damage is a clue to the nature of the stranger/s; aggressive and/or drunk, perhaps. (It was the tail end of Australia Day, the Hobart Regatta and Chinese New Year.)
3. The difficult task of removing some of the flooring, using two screwdrivers abandoned at the scene, is a clue that the stranger/s were looking for something. The aggression exhibited could have been caused perhaps by a combination of frustration (at not finding it) and alcohol.
4. Her visit to Bunnings, very clear in her statement made a day later, was dismissed and ridiculed by the prosecution because she wasn't seen on any of the CCTV cameras at the store. She lied, Mr Ellis said - he said it several times. Bunnings was mentioned dozens of times during the trial. As if it mattered. He treated her claim as if it were a claim for an alibi, which it clearly was not. But he planted that seed in the jury's mind, central to the Crown's case. The prosecution's case actually suggested that Sue Neill-Fraser returned to *Four Winds* around midnight to execute her plan to murder Bob Chappell. (Or was it? The judge and the defence weren't clear themselves about this. See details in the 'Could the jury have got it wrong' chapter.)

Example from transcript - Mr Ellis closing statement:

> *Why did she feel inspired to ring her daughter and her mother in rapid succession at about a quarter past, twenty past nine on the 26th, if not to bolster the lie that she was at Bunnings until around about its closing time, which I suggest she expected it to be not six o'clock as told to her by police but nine o'clock, why else would you ring up your mother – your old mother, at that time of night?*

The judge helped in his summing up:

> *Now there is...a situation when you may use a lie as evidence of guilt. Now the Crown says that these circumstances apply – the Crown says that Ms Neill-Fraser lied in relation to the trip to Bunnings that she said she made on the afternoon of Australia Day...*
>
> *The judge outlines the importance of the Bunnings visit, while (inadvertently no doubt) exposing the absurdity of the Crown's attempt to confuse her claim with a claim for an alibi in the minds of members of the jury:*
>
> *In relation to the trip to Bunnings, Ms Neill-Fraser's case is that although she said on a number of occasions that she'd been to Bunnings on the afternoon of Australia Day, that that was an honest mistake. She'd confused the day an earlier day when she'd been to Bunnings with Australia Day when in fact she hadn't been to Bunnings but that she wasn't lying it was an honest mistake. Now the Crown says that she must have known where she really was on Australia Day. The Crown says that her explanation that she'd made a mistake is*

implausible. The Crown says that what she said about the trip to Bunnings was not consistent and that she tailored what she was telling people about the trip to Bunnings to fit the known information; for example, about the closing time of Bunnings, and that she – that you can be satisfied, you should be satisfied that she wasn't making a mistake she was lying to give herself an alibi, to put herself at a distance from the Four Winds and to – and Mr Chappell...in relation to Bunnings, was it a mistake arising from confusion? You must consider whether, if they were lies, the lies related to a material issue, some fact or circumstance connected with the killing of Mr Chappell. You – you must consider whether the – the telling of the lie, if there was a lie, reveals a knowledge of the crime or of some aspect of it, and whether the motive for telling for the lie was a fear of the truth or a realisation of guilt.

5. The presentation of her statement - its detail and its overall tone - is a strong clue to her knowing nothing of what happened to Bob Chappell. Taken as a whole, the statement can not be reconciled with the illogical and unproven proposition that she murdered Chappell, damaged their new yacht and tried to sink it, on the night of January 26/27, 2009.

Instead of properly assessing and following up these clues, the police focused on Neill-Fraser as their only suspect. TasPol finally arrested her on August 10, 2009. It took over a year to get to court, while she was confined in jail.

At the trial, Det. Sgt. Conroy gave the following evidence under examination by DPP Tim Ellis SC, about Neill-Fraser's inspection of *Four Winds* in the company of Conroy, on the afternoon of January 27 - the very day the disappearance was discovered, when the police considered it a mystery not a murder.

ELLIS: *Did she note anything about the floor?*
CONROY: *She did. The floor was – like only – the floor wasn't screwed – wasn't down to the ground it was opened it, there were holes – boards had been lifted up and she stated that they should have been screwed down and that her partner, Mr Chappell, wouldn't have done that, wouldn't have unscrewed them.*

ELLIS: *Did someone talk about drugs being on board or a possibility of it?*
CONROY: *Yes. It was mentioned to me in my initial briefing that the vessel had possibly been entered on two occasions, at least two occasions previously. Whilst down in the saloon the accused made mention of the break-ins and possible relationship to it. It was apparent to her that something heavy may have been lifted out. And that she believed it was drug smugglers and that Mr Chappell may have been on board when they came back to the boat.*

In the preceding 20 months, the police had spent enormous effort and resources (including bugging the Neill-Fraser house) investigating HER, without any clues having been found pointing TO her. They spent much less effort - in some cases none - on following up any other leads. (See Investigating the Investigators)

THE ABANDONED DINGHY

An unidentified grey dinghy which was seen tied up to Four Winds at 3.55pm on Australia Day, remains a mystery.

Police Inspector Powell, who led the investigation, dismissed the relevance of the grey dinghy altogether. Interviewed on Eve Ash's documentary, *Shadow of Doubt*, he said: "When people see a vessel on the water, like a dinghy, particularly ah, in dusk or darkness, sometimes white looks like grey with the reflection off the water. So.... We're more than happy that any discrepancies in the description of any dinghy that was seen is not, not an issue for us." Dusk was hours away. He also told the filmmaker: "I guess the important thing is that nobody, um, else came forward to say 'I was out in the dinghy'." No, especially not if they were up to no good.

Although dismissed as a lead, it came to be useful against Neill. From the transcript of Shadow of Doubt:

Narrator: Sue believed that she left the Four Winds in the early afternoon. Two – thirty-ish. Now the police came to her and said 'We have a witness that's come forward and seen THE dinghy, no spefics as to the dinghy, but THE dinghy, at the Four Winds at five to four. And it was very deliberatly put to her that it was her dinghy. At no time was it made clear to her that the appearance of the dinghy, as described by the witness, was completely different...that it was clearly not her dinghy. Now she of course accepted the word of the police that they must be right and figured she must have made a mistake, that maybe she was there later.

From Mr Ellis' opening at the trial, attempting to attack Neill-Fraser's credibility:

Witnesses "*had told police that they'd seen Four Winds on its mooring at four o'clock in the afternoon on the 26th and an inflatable dinghy had been tied up alongside on the port side. As the water was choppy they noticed it, it was moving around a lot, and when these two detectives on the 5th February put these observations of witnesses to Ms Neill-Fraser her story shifted, and you'll hear this isn't the only time that her story shifts when other evidence inconsistent with it is put to her. She said – I mean obviously given that there was a dinghy alongside it she must have still been on board and that she'd stayed there longer than she thought...*"

And a little later:

"On the 4th March she, Ms Neill-Fraser, agreed to a video recorded interview with police.. She read over her previous statements and she said that they were correct, although she may have stayed longer on the boat than she'd previously indicated. Now remember, police had told her that the dinghy had been seen at about four o'clock."

Mr Ellis later characterises the vaguest of witness testimonies as if it were robust and probative - dinghy and all:

"So there we have it, a man just on his own, no connection with this case, and he sees inflatable dinghy, an outboard motor, a single person in it at about half past eleven, twelve o'clock on Australia Day evening heading out to where the Four Winds was."

That was all the 'evidence' Mr Ellis had that Neill-Fraser was returning to *Four Winds* ... to murder Bob Chappell. And it turned out that the 'single person' in the dinghy was a man, later identified as Grant Maddock. The two dinghies had merged into one thus giving the jury entirely the wrong impression.

Curiously, another witness, local businessman Gary Smith, reported seeing the grey dinghy ("pretty scruffy looking") in the days leading up to Australia Day, at the rocks where the Four Winds white and blue dinghy, 'Quicksilver' on its side, was found. "It was just a grey one. It wasn't on the beach. It was half way out where the rocks … near the rowing sheds there. … quite a few days as if someone was using it, and leaving it there, and then coming back for it."

They never did.

INVESTIGATING THE INVESTIGATORS

Between the appeal hearing in March and the handing down of the decision in November, in the afternoon of August 31, 2021,Tasmanian Legislative Council member the Hon. Michael Gaffney MLC (Ind), Member for Mersey, devoted his first adjournment speech in 13 years to her case, "first, to bring us together to right a wrong and secondly to have the Attorney-General join us in that quest," tabling the Etter/Selby documents, giving them Parliamentary privilege. (Needless to say, the Attorney-General ignored the documents, even when, some months later, prompted by this author to comment on them.)

The Etter/Selby documents comprise a large and comprehensive series of reports into the failures of TasPol's investigation following the disappearance of Bob Chappell.

Gaffney told this author: "After reading the material received from Lara Giddings, Barbara Etter and Hugh Selby - all of whom I respect - I felt, (perhaps intuitively), that something wasn't right. All MLCs were asked to do whatever they could to keep SNF (and her supporters') dreams alive. One of the things I could do was to present an adjournment speech to assist in keeping the SNF case alive."

Extract from Gaffney's speech:

None of us can ignore these papers establish a miscarriage of justice, now that we are aware of the following issues:

1. An inadequate investigation and tunnel vision by police, which led to obvious lines of inquiry being ignored or barely followed up.

2. Police failure to provide to the Office of the Director of Public Prosecutions (ODPP) the full disclosure of all relevant information.

3. Failures within the ODPP to ensure that their Director and the Defence received all the material supplied by the police.

4. False evidence being put before the jury.

5. A 'conflict of interest' within the ODPP so that personal interests have interfered with the proper conduct of the case.

6. An acquiescence in delay that entailed that Ms Neill-Fraser's application for leave to appeal took over three years.

7. Further delays so that the prisoner then waited almost another two years to have her appeal heard.

8. Despite several sound appeal grounds being available, the March appeal was run on one issue only, for which the only witness - a young woman - was not adequately prepared, managed or supported. During cross-examination her evidence was 'abandoned' by those who had intended to rely upon it.

9. The Appeal court being misled in final submissions by an incorrect answer from the DPP about the significance of the sighting of another dinghy, a grey dinghy, alongside the yacht at a critical time.

The Etter/Selby Report - Extracts:

Barbara Etter APM (Australian Police Medal) is a former Assistant Commissioner of Police (including Corruption Prevention and Investigation in WA), now a non-practicing solicitor and she was the inaugural CEO of the Tasmanian Integrity Commission. She was Sue Neill-Fraser's solicitor from October 2012 until mid 2017.

Hugh Selby headed a police complaints body. He has both prosecuted and defended indictable matters.

The 55 page report analyses and dissects the police investigation into Meaghan Vass and what police knew or should have known and should have disclosed to the Crown and defence counsel.

The impact of non-disclosure – from the report

From the Etter/Selby report tabled in parliament:

"The results of the non-disclosure of relevant material were that:

1. The Crown, the Defence, and the trial judge were misled as to the availability to the SNF defence at trial of a viable (not ephemeral) alternative hypothesis, namely that a person or persons, not being Sue Neill-Fraser, caused Chappell's disappearance (and presumed death).

2. While the issue as to Meaghan Vass being on the yacht (she said she hadn't been on the yacht) as argued in the Court of Appeal and later in the High Court did not amount, at that time, to a 'point of substance' (as found by the High Court in September 2012 on the leave to appeal application), it is clear from what follows that it was and is now a significant 'point of substance'. The reason it was not a point of substance previously is because police were incompetent.

The reason that Justice Blow and the subsequent Appeal Courts did not find the MV evidence sufficiently weighty to warrant her recall at the trial or thereafter to order a retrial is wholly and solely because of inexcusable police failure, **first as to investigation and secondly by their lack of proper disclosure to the Crown.**

This paper demonstrates **a point of substance** that, if known at the time, would either have altered the trial outcome or been of great significance in any appeal.

3. The police disinterest in Ms Vass may be explained by **an early decision by them** to discount any allegation that someone other than Sue Neill-Fraser was responsible for Chappell's disappearance and presumed death. This approach required ignoring any suggestion that some other person or persons had gone aboard the yacht. The obvious reason for such an incursion would be to break in to take food, alcohol or any valuables. This decision should be considered in the context of the following:

10 January 2009 when Sue-Neil Fraser makes a diary entry about a possible break in or illegal access of the Four Winds;

27 January 2009 when Peter Lorraine has a phone chat with TASPOL officer Sinnitt and describes a dinghy that is NOT the Four Winds' dinghy;

27 January 2009 when Grant Maddock, a local yachtsman living on his yacht in the vicinity of Four Winds, speaks with police at the low loading dock at Constitution Dock. He speaks to Conroy [who was in charge of the investigation] (and even emails him photos of the Four Winds immediately prior to that day - T 199 leave to appeal hearing 1 November 2017) but Conroy never contacts him again (see leave to appeal hearing T 198-199 and 205 1 November 2017);

28 January 2009 when Phillip Triffett contacted police 'providing information about the yacht and Ms Fraser' (see Police Investigation Log);

31 January 2009 when Peter Lorraine meets Conroy who has him sign up to a statement that has him seeing the Four Winds' dinghy. Sinnitt's contemporaneous notes of Lorraine's initial evidence that describe a very different sort of dinghy were available to Conroy;

4. Thereafter police have the crime scene/forensic document examiner provide **inconsistent statements** (see Appendix C to [their] paper) in an effort to substantiate a claim that Sue Neill-Fraser had 'doctored' her diary to insert a false 'break in' claim."

The lengthy and detailed submission by Etter & Selby provides a helpful chronology and itemises investigation failures into the disappearance and presumed death of Bob Chappell, whose body has never been found. Some of the failures listed include:

"His life partner was convicted of his murder because the police:

Failed to make any inquiries among the locals and boaties about theft from moored boats. If they did make inquiries then they failed to disclose them. But by June 2012 they admit to knowledge of her associates and their theft from boats (see above);

Allowed the Crown to suggest at trial that the accused had 'fabricated' an entry in her diary about unauthorised access to the Four Winds just a couple of weeks before the Australia Day tragedy when they knew that their forensic evidence did not support that suggestion, and when they should have known, and perhaps did know, about the pilfering from boats;

Put it about that the teenage **Vass' DNA** was left there by someone else via secondary transfer when they should have known that it was **left by her**;

Gave incomplete and misleading evidence at trial that Chappell's blood was in the yacht's dinghy.

A key concern highlighted is the lack of independence of Forensic Science Service Tasmania (FSST) which is corroborated by the conduct of one of their staff at the trial who failed to mention that all the tests done in that laboratory showed that there was no blood in the yacht's dinghy. The Police Investigation Log (PIL) for 16 April 2009 records comments of this scientist that the tests for blood in the dinghy "did not work" [which implies the tests were negative for blood, not positive. There were no positive results]. The improper collaboration between TasPol and FSST is further shown by September 2014 correspondence from Barbara Etter that raised bona fide technical questions addressed to the Director of FSST being dismissively replied to by a senior member of police command.

WHY ....

The Etter/Selby submission puts forward a number of questions that challenge the competence of the police investigation - here are some of them:

- Why is there no supervision, management or leadership evident in this matter? (An RTI request by Etter in 2012 revealed that there were no written records of any directions given by senior officers during the investigation and no records of a briefing of the Commander by the lead Detective as noted on the Investigation Log for 2 March 2009 as the briefing was verbal and there were no written records. When notes or records of other key briefings were requested, advice was provided to Etter that no records were kept of such meetings and the decisions had been recorded on a whiteboard i.e. "no permanent record exists").
- Where are the necessary file notes, diary entries, policy files and critical decision logs (or similar)?

- What further guidance or advice was given to Sinnitt by FSST personnel?
- If secondary transfer (of the Vass DNA) was a possibility why was there no questioning of those documented as coming on board the *Four Winds* as to how they may have come into contact with a significant biological sample (urine, vomit, blood etc) belonging to MV? (See 2010 trial T 788 for 30 September 2010)
- Why is there no analysis of the outcomes of the investigation by Sinnitt?
- Why is there no investigation report or even a memorandum to more senior officers in Operation Ransack?
- Why is there no memorandum or report for the ODDP on the issue?
- What Quality Assurance (QA) or review of the investigation into MV and the DNA took place? What QA or independent review was undertaken of Operation Ransack?
- Why are the relevant staff and residents of Mara House not spoken to about when MV returned to Mara House on 27 January 2009 (as noted by Sinnitt) and her condition, state of mind, any comments on where she had been etc?
- Why was there not further investigation when the address she had given for the evening at Mt Nelson was found to be a non-existent address?
- Why were mobile phone records of Sam Devine not checked when he and MV were known associates and his mobile number was on record in January 2009?
- Why were mobile phone records of MV for the number clearly listed in the disclosure folder including on a Detention record in February 2010 not checked?

- Why were the identified owners of the three mobiles that texted the Meaghan Vass mobile number on 26 and 27 January (that was checked by police) not spoken to and asked the reason for their contact with MV?
- Why was Sam Devine not investigated when he was a documented criminal associate of MV (in January 2009), particularly when Mara House records indicated that MV was spending the night at Sam's place?
- Why did police claim that the diary entry of Sue Neill-Fraser for 10 January 2009 in relation to unlawful trespass and interference with the yacht was false?
- Why did they continue with this allegation in light of the statement of forensic document examiner Constable Tony Fox dated 4 March 2009 prior to trial re document examination?
- Why were people living on the Marieville Esplanade foreshore or on their yachts in the vicinity of the Four Winds on the night in question (such as Grant Maddock) not carefully and thoroughly questioned about their observations, movements and any information about theft, trespass and break-ins, as well as the theft of dinghies?"

LEGAL PRECEDENT

The High Court's decision in *Penney v R* [1998] HCA 51;(1998) 155 ALR 605; (1998) 72 ALJR 1316 is instructive, especially the following, from the leading judgment of Callinan J who discussed the significance of a "defective" police investigation:

> "...there may be cases in which deficiencies in the investigation might be of such significance to a particular case as a whole that the accused will be entitled to an acquittal or

a retrial. But that will all depend on the facts of the particular case."

Regard should also be had to the High Court decision in *AB v CD and others*, 2018 HCA 58, This decision is illuminating because, inter alia, the full court said,

> Victoria Police were guilty of reprehensible conduct in knowingly encouraging EF to do as she did and were involved in sanctioning atrocious breaches of the sworn duty of every police officer to discharge all duties imposed on them faithfully and according to law without favour or affection, malice or ill-will[2]. As a result, the prosecution of each Convicted Person was corrupted in a manner which debased fundamental premises of the criminal justice system…[10]

They were considering the case of a defence solicitor in Melbourne turned police informant; however, the remarks have a somewhat wider application. *Penney's* time may be nigh.

The authors (Etter/Selby) assert that the police deficiencies described in the paper combine to realise the facts to which Justice Callinan was referring as justifying at least a retrial, and possibly an acquittal. His Honour's dicta have been cited in cases around Australia, including in Tasmania by (the trial judge, now Chief Justice) Blow CJ in *Pike v Lusted* [2017] TASSC 46 at [13].

The following revealing quote from Detective Inspector Peter Powell on 27 June 2012, while being filmed by Eve Ash appears on the very first page of the report:

> … and certainly Meaghan Vass had some associations with some young male offenders, underage offenders, that have been in the past guilty from breaking into boat yards and stealing things off boats.

It is revealing, and it is important because it is an admission that the police knew about break ins, break ins that they avoided making proper inquiries about. This line of inquiry is so obvious that its neglect says a great deal about the problems with the police investigation.

Sue Neill-Fraser at 3-4 years (Edinburgh, Scotland)

Helen Neill-Fraser returning to Hobart from the U.K. with Sue and her brother Patrick ('The Mercury' 1957-8)

Sue outside London (1970)

Sue riding 'Hi!' cross country event at Old Beach Tasmania (late 1970's)

Sailing with children near Bruny Island, Derwent Estuary, Tas (1989-90)

Setting off over the Zoji La Pass, Himalayas (1988)

Trekking in Ladahk, Northern India (1988)

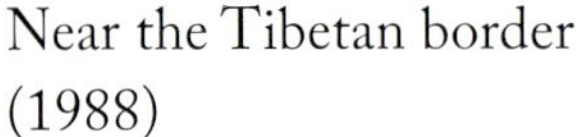

Near the Tibetan border (1988)

Sue with her father 'Bronte' in Jersey, Channel Islands (1988)

Sue and Bob skiing at Ben Lomond (1990)

Bob with parrots, family trip to Bali (1998)

Bob, Sue, Emma and Sarah. Family holiday in Bali (1998)

Sue with family members 'Charlie', 'Wretched' and 'Herman' back veranda West Hobart (1996-8).

Bob cooking at a family barbecue, West Hobart (2004-5)

Cartoon by Rosemary Phelps, member of The Sue Neill-Fraser Support Group

COULD THE JURY HAVE GOT IT WRONG?

Juries are full of humans. Fallible, often under stress, especially in trials of serious crime, men and women collectively uninformed in law, forensic science or other relevant disciplines. Juries ingest what the prosecution and defence feeds them. Having served on a jury, I know from first-hand experience how hard it is to sift evidence, to assess witnesses and to avoid the natural bias of the police, the pleadings of the accused and to weigh court theatrics against what the lawyers say are cold facts.

Juries can be misled by confusing evidence, by practiced prosecutors swaying the jury with slanted argument or pleas to emotion - and even by the jury's own conscious or unconscious misconceptions or prejudices. The Lindy Chamberlain trial is a good example of a jury getting it wrong - because they were told 'wrongs'.

And it isn't just what they are told but how. Observers on the public benches at the trial of Sue Neill-Fraser report being shocked at some of the proceedings. Lynn Giddings, who had sat through the trial and made copious notes, describes it as having been "all theatre". She said the experience drained her confidence in the justice system. (Giddings became a central figure in the Sue Neill-Fraser Support Group.)

In Volume 1 (Chapter 11) I show with three examples how prosecutors can secure (wrongful) convictions in cases relying solely on circumstantial evidence by applying three 'imperatives'.

IMPERATIVE 1 Establish and/or embellish conflict between accused and victim and/or potential motive, however slight.

IMPERATIVE 2 Speculate on a scenario describing the murder in detail, even if implausible. 'Sell' the story to the jury.

IMPERATIVE 3 Present any forensic and/or expert witness evidence angled to implicate the accused, playing on judge and jury ignorance about forensic and other technical or scientific matters.

In the Sue Neill-Fraser trial, there was the instance of Neill-Fraser, the accused, wrongly attributed to have had an argument with the deceased ('the murder victim') on the very day he disappeared from his yacht. The jury were so led to believe - a clear case of 'imperative one' in action. However, it wasn't the accused but Ann Sanchez, sister of the deceased (Bob Chappell) who was overheard arguing loudly on the Hobart wharf that day. Actually, even the day was wrong. Here is an excerpt from Volume 1 Chapter 3 (quoting the transcript) on the subject:

Prosecutor: You've said that it's more likely that the woman that you saw that you believe was speaking in a raised voice to Mr Chappell was going to another yacht, why is that more likely?

Mrs Zochling: Well because the woman I saw originally with Mr Chappell was - I thought was a blonde - a blonde ash hair, shoulder length hair, and when I -
Prosecutor: Right.

Mrs Zochling: And when I saw the television - ... sorry, when I came to the Court here and saw that the lady in the box there had black hair - ... that's the reason I thought that I had the wrong person.

Here is what happened next:

MR ELLIS SC: I see. I think we might have a picture of the lady you might have seen – sorry, your Honour, just bear with me –
HIS HONOUR: P50 – you might be thinking about P50, tab 5 in the blue folder?

MR ELLIS SC: Yes, thank you. (Resuming): Well maybe P50 number 1. Can you see the woman that you saw there?.......

MRS ZOCHLING: No the woman that – the woman – it – the one in the front here –
MR ELLIS SC: Mm, I'm just asking you if you see her there?.......
MRS ZOCHLING: It doesn't seem to be – oh sorry, would you ask me the question again?
MER ELLIS SC: Yes, without – without looking at the accused, do you see the woman there that you saw?.......
MRS ZOCHLING: Yeah, but that's – the woman – In photograph 1........– that I saw had blond hair.
MR ELLIS SC: Blond hair?
MRS ZOCHLING: Yeah, blond ashen hair.
MR ELLIS SC: Absolutely blond?
MRS ZOCHLING: No, no, no, no, ashen blond, sort of – I don't know – it just – I didn't really take much notice, but it certainly wasn't that colour.
MR ELLIS SC: Right. It was black?.......

MRS SANCHEZ: Well I – when I – well I don't know, black, whatever, I saw it on TV.
MR ELLIS SC: Yeah, what you saw on TV. thank you, your Honour.
HIS HONOUR: Yes, all right, thank you, Ms Zochling, you're free to go.

Whatever impression the jury was left with is unclear, but the prosecution was identifying Sue Neill-Fraser as having a public shouting match with Bob Chappell, to emphasise their conflicted relationship.

As an observer (who wishes to remain anonymous) at the trial later put in writing to this author:

> *What the court and the jury failed to hear was that Mrs Zochling remained in the precincts of the court after giving her evidence under oath. At the next adjournment she spoke with a family member outside the court and pointed to Bob Chappell's sister, Ann Sanchez, as the woman she had seen on the beach speaking in a loud voice. Ann Sanchez, who was visiting from Ecuador, having married an Ecuadorian, fits Mrs Zochling's description of an ash blond with shoulder length hair. This information was relayed by the family member to the defence counsel's assistant and, at some stage, Ann Sanchez herself informed Detective Inspector Peter Powell, who was in charge of the case. All to no avail.*
>
> *What the jury did not hear was that Ann Sanchez was not on the beach with her brother on that Australia Day; it was the previous day, 25 January, when the family, including Ann Sanchez, sailed on the yacht to Bruny Island for the day. It is a case of wrong person, wrong day. This conflicting and*

incorrect evidence cannot be used as a valid point for appeal as it was available at the time of the trial and was overlooked.

There was no opportunity for the jury to board and examine *Four Winds*, the yacht on which the prosecution claimed the murder had occurred. The judge was told it was not necessary.

From the transcript (Gunson is the defence barrister) - jury absent:

MR GUNSON SC: I have prepared and provided to the Crown the accused's list of places for the jury view. My friend has the list. The only question, I suppose, is when is it practical to do that?
HIS HONOUR: Is – is everything on this list able to be viewed from the land?
MR GUNSON SC: Yes, no one needs to go to sea, your Honour.

It is arguable that Gunson should have been the one to insist on taking the jury on board. Instead, his flippant remark obscures an important error of judgement on his part. The yacht was the supposed crime scene, and uniquely available to view and explore thoroughly, when the trial began, 20 months after the event, tied up just a short distance from the court. The impact on the jury would have been profound, when they would recall during the trial the narrow confines of the cabin and the steep stairs leading down to the lowest deck where Chappell was working. Could anyone - let alone a middle aged woman with a bad back - have done what the prosecution put to them (all without evidence), that she killed him below decks and dragged him up to dispose of the body via the dinghy. The jury would also have seen that getting a body from the top deck into the dinghy would be a marvellous feat for anyone. In the dark. Without capsizing the little dinghy. With a fire extinguisher roped to the body. And then getting herself into it....

This viewing - by itself - may well have seeded reasonable doubt (or perhaps total incredulity of the prosecution's speculation) in the minds of the jury.

Gunson wanted to make the closing address to the jury as the last thing they heard, so he advised his client not to call any witnesses to testify. That gave him the right to close. Was that the right thing to do? Neill-Fraser had explained the history concerning the damaged Phillip Triffett relationship and their fear of him, to which Gunson replied, 'Don't worry, they wouldn't dare use him'. Gunson is accused of flagrant incompetence by Tony Jacobs (see Chapter *Correct this injustice, the product of our Tasmanian legal family*) and failed to disclose to his client his close relationship with the DPP, Tim Ellis SC.

During the trial, Ellis referred to her as a liar multiple times, dealt with her aggressively and broke the fair trial rules in doing so. The judge did nothing to restrain him. The Prosecution Policy and Guidelines, states: "advocacy must be conducted ... temperately and with restraint." & "Prosecutors must not, by language or other conduct, seek to inflame or bias the court against the accused"

At one point during his cross examination of Sue Neill-Fraser, Ellis made a point of giving the jury the impression that she was trying to cover up for her DNA being at what he claimed to be the crime scene by touching the winches: "And so that when your DNA turns out to be on the winch handle, then that's perfectly explicable because you did pick them up in the presence of the police..." Defence counsel could have (should have?) sought the judge's intervention on this, to advise the jury to ignore the inference of tampering with evidence, given that the yacht was her property and her DNA would be found everywhere - whether she touched the winches on that day or not.

The jury was left with a biased view of her character, in the wake of the prosecution's character assassination of her. There was no-one to remind the jury that she had never been violent, had no criminal record and was a loving partner to the man she was accused of murdering. Her calm demeanour in court was a reflection of her stoic character. She didn't break down and cry - as she was expected to in court, just as she might have been expected to when making her statement to Detective Sergeant Conroy on February 28, 2009, the day after her Bob went missing in mysterious circumstances.

"Our contemporaries, including juries, are more disposed to believe accounts that are expressed with emotional power. Persons who express things stoically, in a matter-of-fact manner, are less likely to be believed," observed Peter Murphy (Quadrant, Dec. 28, 2018). [Author Peter Murphy is Professor of Arts and Society at James Cook University.]

Near the end of the trial (on Oct. 13, 2010), there was an illuminating exchange (with jury absent) between His Honour and Counsel:

MR ELLIS SC: It was put by my learned friend that it was only in closing that the prosecution, or the prosecutor, or probably the evil DPP, first advanced that Ms Neill-Fraser went out at midnight and committed this crime. It's not a matter of first advancing, I've never advanced it, it's mischaracterising what I have advanced. The crime may well have been committed when Ms Neill-Fraser went out at midnight..

HIS HONOUR: But you've never said whether it was in the afternoon or in the middle of the night.
MR ELLIS SC: No, that's right, I've never advanced that as a theory.
HIS HONOUR: Right. Mr Gunson, what do you say?
MR GUNSON SC: I must say I was left with the impression that the Crown case was predicated on the basis that there'd been this furtive midnight visit and the first time I think it was put on any other basis was in the course of the submissions today that to the effect the possibility was it happened during the course of the afternoon and she had gone out there at midnight to dispose of the body because of the telephone call had in some way – my words – spooked her. I must say I've been always left with the impression that the Crown case was on that basis, that is the first basis that the event in question had occurred at night and I think that was the way it was basically – I just can't –
HIS HONOUR: Well that might have been something that you read into the Crown case that Mr Ellis didn't say. I've certainly understood as the trial progressed that a killing during the afternoon is something consistent with the Crown case.
MR GUNSON SC: I must confess I hadn't picked that up until the very last – well there were mild suggestions of it, particularly in cross-examination, but the final proposition was advanced only today. But I started the case with and have continued through at least until the point of cross-examination on the basis that the crime was committed sometime late at night. But that's probably my error, just as the case unfolded. But he's right, he didn't ever say that.

If defence counsel was confused about the time of the murder as claimed by the Crown, was the jury also confused? Was that confusion the result of the absence of any evidence as to when and how the murder was committed and by whom?

Defence counsel and the trial judge were also confused about 'blood in the dinghy'.

CT 1486 HIS HONOUR, COUNSEL, JURY ABSENT – SUBMISSIONS, PRIOR TO SUMMING UP, 13/10/2010

MR ELLIS SC: The next point is, it was attributed to me that I said it was Mr Chappell's blood in the dinghy. Now I don't believe I did.
MR GUNSON SC: Yes, you did.
MR ELLIS SC: Okay – I don't know why I'd say it
HIS HONOUR: – Well – -
MR ELLIS SC: – because I've never believed it.
HIS HONOUR: In opening.
MR GUNSON SC: Yeah.
MR ELLIS SC: Oh in opening –
MR GUNSON SC: Yes, in opening.
MR ELLIS SC: Oh okay, I abandon that, if I said it in opening.
HIS HONOUR: All right. Well I'll do nothing about that point. What's the next point?

Could the jury have also thought the prosecutor was claiming it was Bob Chappell's blood in the dinghy…the dinghy in which he claimed Neill-Fraser had disposed of the bloody body? Had His Honour clarified that matter, could the jury have held a reasonable doubt about Neill-Fraser's guilt? Why didn't he "do anything about that point"? Why didn't Gunson for the defence? The DPP accepted that he might have said it in his opening address – yet he never believed it. Why did he show the jury a photo of the luminol-stained dinghy, when explaining that luminol was a test for blood (without adding it was a preliminary test and also responsive to about a hundred other substances)?

By the time the Hobart Mercury front page screamed THERE WAS NO BLOOD (David Killick reporting on the appeal underway, March 9, 2018), it was too late; the verdict had been delivered years before.

THE CARNAGE OF THE SECOND APPEAL

After the legal mess of the 2010 trial and the various errors of judgement in the first appeal in 2011, the second appeal degenerated into carnage.

The appeal was heard March 1- 3, 2021, six years after the further right to appeal legislation was introduced in 2015 by then Attorney-General the late Vanessa Goodwin. On November 30, 2021, the judges dismissed the appeal in a 2:1 decision.

In the lead-up to the hearing, a former State and Federal court judge familiar with the case told this author that the Tasmanian judges (Justices Helen Wood, Stephen Estcourt and Robert Pearce) to hear the appeal should disqualify themselves and be replaced by interstate judges. They may be called on to consider matters concerning the trial judge, who is now their Chief Justice, Alan Blow AO. This would put them in a conflicted position.

A secondary consideration, said the judge, is the closely knit nature of Tasmania's legal fraternity. This is not to question the ethics of those involved, but the silken threads of friendship are recognised as a reality of the human condition and could well make the public uneasy - especially so in this matter. No change was made.

Key witness - Meaghan Vass

Vass was always a central figure in this case, her DNA at the crime scene having placed her there. A vulnerable young woman, she had been an even more vulnerable homeless 16 year old at the time. That she had been too scared to admit being an eye witness to the fight that ended in death is understandable – and the black hole that sucks up the entire case. (Vass has since become a mother and continues to live in Hobart.)

She had agreed to give evidence at the March 2021 appeal to confirm under oath in court the contents of her affidavit that she was indeed on board the Four Winds … the key to Sue Neill-Fraser's freedom. Two years earlier, she had made the same (tearful) admission on *60 Minutes.*

It started well enough on Monday, March 1, 2021, with Robert Richter KC taking her through her testimony. The courtroom was filled to capacity, mostly with family and supporters, eager to see the prospect of the truth coming out.

Then came the carnage. The front page of The Mercury was devoted to the headline "SAM DID IT" as it reported what Vass told the court in her eye witness account of the fight between her then boyfriend Sam Devine and Bob Chappell, who had been below decks when the youngsters boarded – unaware of his presence on board, thanks to the absence of the yacht's dinghy (taken ashore by Sue Neill-Fraser earlier).

The publication of Sam's name shattered Vass' sense of security and her trust in the undertaking by her then (temporary) solicitor Stuart Wright, that his name would be suppressed. Vass was a nervous wreck that Tuesday morning, seen on a video screen in the main courtroom, alternately sobbing and twisting her body in mental and physical anguish. It was a traumatic experience for the entire court, as the DPP began his cross examination. Daryl Coates SC was relentless in exploiting her vulnerability and her distressing emotional unravelling to achieve his objective: damage or destroy the credibility of her testimony in the appeal court.

Not once did he seem to acknowledge, let alone sympathise with, her anguish, her tears, her stress. Not once did he approach her with the faintest kindness of one human to another. Not once did he treat her as a vulnerable and visibly distressed young woman. She was an obstacle to be bulldozed out of his way to a court room victory.

Under his barrage and desperate to get out of there as she indicated, Vass – head bowed, responses monosyllabic, agreed to all his propositions that negated her testimony from the day before.

But no lawyer in the court - and no judge, either - acknowledged that her testimony on that Tuesday - conflicting with the day before - was being given under duress. Her confidence had been betrayed - by another lawyer, and she felt her safety was at risk. Justice was not served that day.

Was it the truth that the Crown was seeking? Or to protect the conviction. I think most people know the answer. There in Hobart's Supreme Court, the altar of justice one would think, the onus of proof was again flipped; Meaghan Vass' evidence was required to prove Sue Neill-Fraser's innocence. Just as it had been at trial, where in the absence of any primary evidence, Neill-Fraser was effectively required to prove her innocence. Justice was not served that day, either.

Robin Bowles, author of *Death on the Derwent* (Scribe) one of three books on the Sue Neill-Fraser case, has noted that Vass "was persuaded to tell the truth believing she could swear an affidavit and she'd only ever have to answer questions on the things in that affidavit, but of course under our adversarial legal system the DPP could attempt to elicit much more VITAL info, such as how tall the men on the boat with her were, how old, eye colour, etc! It's a wonder he didn't ask what they had for breakfast!!" True enough, Coates managed to so discombobulate Vass that she was in a trance of submission.

What she didn't reveal, but other sources have confirmed to the author, Vass received several death threats, not only but also immediately after the SAM DID IT headline.

The aftermath interview

A traumatised and betrayed Meaghan Vass sought safety and comfort among her close friends. But she agreed to this written Q&A with the author, a few days after the appeal hearing concluded.

Q1 You were terribly upset in court; what upset you most? Why did you agree to the propositions he put to, contradicting what you had said earlier?

The entire subject makes me upset. I was upset because I was hounded and had words put in my mouth....he (Mr Coates) ***was trying to confuse me and butt in with what he thought and cutting me off. I didn't want the names out in public. I panicked and was so scared. It was all I could think of to do.***

(Meaghan later added:) ***I didn't f....ing murder anybody, why are they treating me like this...so I just wanted to shut it all down and get out of there.***

Q2 Mr Coates SC suggested (among other things) that you probably went on board *Four Winds* a day or two after the murder, probably at Goodwood. What do you say to that?

Mr Coates is wrong. He doesn't want to hear the truth. I know where I was and I know where the boat was and it wasn't at Goodwood. He has a job to do but it's not listening to the truth.

Q3 What would you say now to the court if given a chance?

I'd say it was wrong of the lawyer (Stuart Wright) ***not to suppress my information from the affidavit from 2019 as promised. I'm not crazy and I'm not a liar. I'm telling the truth and no one is listening.***

Q4 Mr Coates also tried to imply that you may have been paid to say you were at the crime scene. What do you say to that?

I was never paid to do anything. 60 mins was also zero dollars, for those implying it wasn't. As if I'd risk implicating myself in something for money if I was no part of it. I was stood over and threatened by people, but not regarding that I was there. They wanted me to make up a big story of how it happened that wasn't true. Karen Keefe was the main one. Telling me to say i was on the piss having a party on the boat with bob when things turned sour. That was bullshit. She is evil. But Jeff thompson (Hobart solicitor) ***has been so good to me. I love jeff. He's such a sweet man who only wants the truth as well.***

Q5 Has anyone at all contacted you since your court appearance?

Yes a few people from Tas Police to ask if I was safe - and mostly people have been ok. I've received nasty messages on facebook which I block.

Q6 You were said to have apologised to Sue Neill-Fraser and her lawyers - is that true? Can you put into words why you felt sorry?

Because I feel like I tried to do what was right but it seemed doomed from the start, from Andy not being allowed (to be her support person in the witness box***), to the suppression etc...I tried again and again to say that the 2019 affidavit was true. Then I spoke with fabiano*** *(Cangelosi, MV's barrister from 2017)* ***about it but by then it was too late. My evidence was not of any use, so they said.***

Q7 Do you feel the need for police protection?

No way. Police protection. That's funny. I don't want them anywhere near me. I don't trust them at all.

Q8 What would you like to see happen next?

I'd like to see the appeal seen for what it was by the judges. Surely they can. I want the lawyer who promised me suppression be reprimanded as he is the only reason things turned out the way they did on the Tuesday.

To everyone. My 2019 60 mins interview + affidavit is true and correct.

Vass also provided the following document:

MV affidavit for attention of Tasmanian Court of Criminal Appeal in case of Sue Neill-Fraser appeal - points to include

I make this sworn statement to confirm the evidence I gave on March 1, 2021 and to retract the evidence I gave on March 2, 2021 in the Supreme Court.

In response to questions from Mr Robert Richter QC, on March 1, I confirmed that the contents of my affidavit of 2019 were true, as were my statements on 60 Minutes, broadcast on March 10, 2019.

I confirmed then and confirm now that I had been on board Four Winds on January 26, 2009.

I confirmed then and confirm now that Sue Neill-Fraser was not present.

I confirmed then and confirm now that I had witnessed a fight break out on board between the males I was with and the older man on board, who I understand was Mr Bob Chappell.

I confirmed then and confirm now the names of the males as stated on my 2019 affidavit on the understanding given to me by Mr Stuart Wright that their names would be suppressed.

The front page headline of the next day's Hobart Mercury stated 'SAM DID IT' in contravention of the undertaking from Mr Stuart Wright, and went on to name the males who accompanied me. Other media also reported the names. The suppression order was then ordered by Justice Wood on March 2, 2021. Too late.

I initiated a formal complaint against Mr Wright with the Legal Profession Board# (Ref: 210043) on 15 March 2021 and I hold him responsible for putting my safety in danger.

Further I accuse him of interfering with the appeal process and perverting the course of justice.

The failure to suppress their names caused me to panic in fear of possible retributions against me, which affected my testimony on March 2 when responding to statements put to me by Mr Coates. I agreed with his propositions out of panic and wish to withdraw them all.

Mr Coates also tried to imply that I may have been paid to say I was at the crime scene. I was never paid to do anything. My 60 Minutes interview was also for zero dollars. As if I'd risk implicating myself in something for money if I was no part of it. I was stood over and threatened by people, who wanted me to make up a big story of how it happened, that wasn't true. [Name supplied] was the main one. Telling me to say I was on the piss having a party on the boat with Bob when things turned sour. That was not true.

In the lead up to the March 1-3, 2021, appeal in Hobart's Supreme Court, Meaghan Vass, her friend and support Andrea 'Andy' Brown, and her newly attached temporary lawyer Stuart Wright met. "It was me, him and Meaghan in the room," Brown recalls. "There was an affidavit from 2012, one from 2019, and all Meaghan said was, "Can you guarantee me, promise me that what's said in these or mentioned about anything in these and the names will not get out to media and it will be kept in here?"

"He stood there with his one hand on one document, one hand on the other, leaned over the table, he goes, 'I can 100% guarantee it, Megan.'" Yet the headline on the front page of the next day's Hobart Mercury proclaimed 'SAM DID IT" *– exactly what Vass was afraid of, her testimony revealing who she was with her at the crime scene, on board the *Four Winds* yacht. The headline made her feel like a target. The court issued a suppression order immediately, but of course, it was too late.

When the author contacted Wright at the time, he declined to comment.

Brown (who jointly filed the complaint) had told the Legal Profession Board in her written reply to Wright's defensive claims: "I received an email from the head reporter from the Hobart Mercury saying he had no idea why there wasn't any suppression and it was a shock that the paper was allowed to print the names but then they had to recant later that evening. … Mr Wright single handedly unravelled that appeal by not protecting his client."

* Sam Devine has not attempted to take legal action (defamation) against either Vass or the Mercury.

The Legal Profession Board complaint

The complaint to the Legal Profession Board was received March 9, 2021; the matter was heard on May 31, 2021, determined on June 7, 2021, and dismissed under S433 (1)(a) – as 'misconceived'.

Below are the relevant paragraphs from the notice of dismissal of the appeal, followed by the author's comments (**in bold**):

39 – "There are no facts before the Board which could establish that the Practitioner was engaged by or on behalf of the Witness to attempt to control the publication of evidence which she might give in the course of the hearing."

No, this is a disturbing mischaracterisation. The Practitioner was not expected to 'control publication of evidence'; the Witness wanted an assurance that the names of those persons who the Witness was going to identify in court would not be made public. As the solicitor helping the Witness

in court, the Practitioner was reasonably expected to act in a professional manner and to perform his service in accordance with court procedures. Suppression orders are fairly common and are not regarded as 'controlling the publication of evidence'.

40 – "It is common ground that prior to the hearing the Complainant had asked the Practitioner whether the statutory declaration made by the Witness would be released by the Court. The Practitioner informed the Complainant that it would not be released. Even if that request was on behalf of the Witness rather than the Complainant, it did not extend to engagement with respect to the suppression of any evidence." No, this is also a disturbing mischaracterisation of the facts. The Practitioner gave "100% guarantee" that the names of those persons who the Witness was going to identify in court would not be made public.

41 – "Further, the material before the Board makes it clear that the only practitioners acting in that capacity before the Court, were those on behalf of the prosecution and of the defendant. The Practitioner was appointed to assist the Witness and the Court, The Practitioner was not entitled to, and had no standing to, make any application with respect to suppression of evidence."

This reads like a transparent attempt to protect the Practitioner from the allegation of professional misconduct. The Board surely knows that as a professional solicitor, the Practitioner would recognise that to give effect to his undertaking he was required to advise the Witness' instructing solicitor, Paul Galbally, of his undertaking to the Witness and to request Galbally to put the request to the bench according to

normal court procedures. At no time did the Practitioner advise the Witness that he could not execute the task requested of him and which he agreed to execute with his own '100% guarantee'.

The Appeal judges' decisions

The appeal concluded on the third day, March 3, 2021. The decision to dismiss was delivered on November 30, 2021, 2:1 with Estcourt J dissenting.

Below are my layman's observations (*in italics)* on Justice Wood's reasons followed by extracts from Justice Estcourt's dissenting reasons:

Justice Wood on occasions appears to be making allowances for 'the Director', eg:

240 Mr Grosser's evidence: the Director took some liberties with the evidence, or perhaps more precisely with the absence of evidence. I am not suggesting deliberately so.

The Director painted generalised scenarios which had not been explored in the evidence.

The Director's scenario strayed away from the evidence into conjecture.

241 The misleading quality of the scenarios - it presented circumstances as giving rise to secondary transfer which had not been canvassed in the evidence and if they had been, would have been heavily qualified. It made it seem that any number of circumstances may feasibly give rise to secondary transfer when that had not been the subject of evidence.

(Could that have misled the jury?)

242 This lack of evidence for generalised scenarios painted by the Director was apparent at the trial, and if the Director crossed the line [*not an assertion that he did?*] in terms of a prosecutor's duty, and in light of the "great trust" that jurors have in prosecution counsel, any unfairness, if it arose, [*not an assertion that it did?*] could have been cured at the time of the trial or could have been the subject of the first appeal.

[Isn't the whole point of a second appeal to deal with unfairness which has not been properly dealt with at trial or on a first appeal?]

318 The jury need not have decided whether Ms Vass's DNA was the result of a direct deposit or secondary deposit in order to have found the appellant guilty. It was entirely open to the jury to be satisfied beyond reasonable doubt of the appellant's guilt and to regard the State's case that the appellant was the perpetrator as an overwhelming case. If the jury made a finding and reached a view about the most feasible causal mechanism for the deposit of Ms Vass's DNA, neither mechanism was inconsistent with the appellant's guilt. *[1 - If so, why was the prosecution so adamant to argue that it was a secondary deposit? 2 – If the jury reached the view that it was a direct deposit, it follows that Vass was at the crime scene; why would the jury not consider that to be a vital fact with profound implications for their verdict?]*

Justice Wood's Conclusion:

319 For the reasons I have given, the evidence of Mr Jones is not fresh, it is not compelling and taking it into account together with the evidence given at the trial, there has not been a substantial miscarriage of justice. The appellant has not established that there is a significant possibility that a jury, acting reasonably,

would have acquitted the appellant had the evidence of Mr Jones been before the jury at her trial. I would dismiss the appeal. [*See comments above*]

Justice Estcourt came to a different conclusion:

The law:

426 The relevant provisions of the Code are set out earlier in my reasons. The question may be distilled as one of whether Mr Jones's evidence concerning the nature and quality of the DNA sample taken from the walkway of the *Four Winds* on 30 January 2009 and as to the likelihood of its secondary transfer, is fresh and compelling evidence within the meaning of s 402A of the Code, and whether if so, that evidence demonstrates a miscarriage of justice.

427 In *Van Beelen v The Queen* [2017] HCA 48, 349 ALR 578, the High Court confirmed that the relevant test for a substantial miscarriage of justice in a case such as the present, is the test laid down in *Mickelberg v The Queen* (1989) 167 CLR 259. That is, whether the court considers that there is a significant possibility that the jury, acting reasonably, would have acquitted the appellant had the fresh evidence been before it at the trial. Counsel on the present appeal were agreed that the *Mickelberg* test was the test to be applied by this Court.

Is the evidence fresh?

430 The appellant relies for this submission on what was said in a joint judgment of the South Australian Court of Criminal Appeal in *R v Keogh (No 2)* [2014] SASCFC 136 at [102] namely:

> "An applicant bears the onus of establishing that evidence relied upon for this purpose is fresh. The question of whether evidence was adduced at trial for the purpose of 353A(6)(a)(i) may be determined by having regard to the transcript of evidence at trial. The requirement in section 353A(6)(a)(ii), that the evidence could not, even with the exercise of reasonable diligence, have been adduced at trial, requires an objective assessment of what the applicant could reasonably be expected to have done in all of the circumstances leading up to and including the trial."

431 The appellant also relies on *R v Drummond (No 2)* [2015] SASCFC 82 at [174] per Peek J, where his Honour said, after reviewing the common law cases as to fresh evidence:
"Of course, the present application is made pursuant to s 353A of the Act and the question of whether the evidence is fresh remains to be answered. However, the above authorities are relevant to that question because, when assessing whether defence counsel used reasonable diligence, one must take into account that counsel is entitled to assume that the prosecution will disclose to the defence relevant evidence and material and, a fortiori, that the prosecution will not lead false or misleading evidence as part of its case. Further, when making an assessment of whether there was reasonable diligence, the court will extend to an accused great latitude.

432 In my view, the relevant opinion evidence of Mr Jones summarised at [34 (a) – (g)] of Brett J's reasons on the leave application set out at [425] above must, in "the circumstances

leading up to and including the trial", be regarded as fresh evidence. It is not suggested that the tests carried out by Mr Jones, including having recourse to the electropherogram, could not have been conducted in 2009. However as I apprehend it, recourse to the electropherogram was not routine and, in my view, it could not reasonably be expected to have been sought out by the accused in all of the circumstances.

433 Notwithstanding the lack of any evidence from trial counsel, it is evident to me from the way Mr Grosser's evidence was led, and objected to, and subsequently cross-examined, that his opinion had not been disclosed to the appellant up until the time that evidence was introduced at trial. Extending "great latitude" it could not, on an objective assessment, fairly be said that "with the exercise of reasonable diligence", Mr Jones's evidence could have been adduced at the trial on behalf of the accused.

434 I accept the submission of Mr Carr in his closing address to this Court, namely:

> "So, when one extends great latitude to defence counsel, looks at the context of this trial with its complexities, its volume of material and so forth, and the stage of the trial when this evidence was led without disclosure, one readily reaches the conclusion, in our submission, that evidence answering or addressing that evidence that was led by the director is fresh."

435 In my view the evidence is fresh within the meaning of s 402A(10)(a) of the Code.

Is the evidence compelling?

437 I will turn in due course to the transcript of all of the evidence of Mr Grosser given at trial that might have enabled those submissions to have been fairly made, but for present purposes I note, as observed by Brett J at [35] of his reasons set out above, that the principal difference between Mr Grosser's evidence at trial and Mr Jones's evidence on the leave application, was that Mr Grosser would not be drawn on an assessment of the likelihood between primary and secondary transfer, whereas Mr Jones was prepared to say that although it depended on the surrounding circumstances, the nature of the DNA profile was not typical of secondary transfer.

442 To my mind, the requirement, as Mr Carr put it for "a concatenation of quite specific circumstances with a very close connection between the picking up of the DNA and its deposit on the deck of the *Four Winds*" is compelling evidence within the meaning of s 402A(10)(b) of the Code.

443 The evidence is clearly reliable and it is substantial given that it is contrary to the way the matter was put to the jury at trial. That evidence would not have allowed Crown counsel to properly put to the jury that the probability was that Ms Vass's DNA was simply somehow picked up anywhere in Hobart, by someone wandering around, then getting in a car, driving to the dock and walking onto the yacht. Again, as Mr Carr submitted to this Court, "[t]hat hypothesis, which was the way that the director deconstructed this pillar of the defence case at trial, is simply not possible on what Mr Jones said ..."

444 Finally, on this issue of whether the evidence is compelling, I am satisfied that in the context of the issues in dispute at the appellant's trial, it would have been highly probative of her case, based as it was on a contended hypothesis that Mr Chappell's death was caused by another person or persons boarding the yacht around the time of his disappearance. It would have cast significant doubt on Ms Vass's denials that she had ever been on board the vessel.

Justice Estcourt's Conclusion

459 Having regard to the evidence at the accused's trial and the closing addresses of counsel and the learned trial judge's summing up, I am of the view, after taking into account the fresh and compelling evidence of Mr Jones, that there has been a substantial miscarriage of justice.

461 Had Mr Jones's evidence been before the jury, the Crown case could not have been left to the jury with the reasonable hypothesis raised by the defence as to Ms Vass being present on the yacht trivialised as it was, as a "red herring". Had the jury been exposed to expert evidence that secondary transfer of Ms Vass's DNA on the sole of someone's shoe would have been a "very rare occurrence" requiring a very specific and immediate concatenation of steps …

463 In my view, on an objective assessment of the record, and recognising the limitations in doing so, after taking into account the fresh and compelling evidence of Mr Jones, there is a significant possibility that the jury, acting reasonably, might have acquitted the appellant had the fresh evidence been before it at the trial.

465 I would uphold the appeal and quash the appellant's conviction for murder.

Edited extracts from legal academic Dr Bob Moles' analysis identifies what he perceives to be disturbing errors that led to the dismissal of the appeal.

Author's note:
The original analysis is almost 9,000 words, and even our edited excerpts (omitting a summary of the case history) run to almost 5,500 words, but the controversial nature and long history of this case warrants such detail.

Leading judgment to dismiss appeal by Wood J
KEY: The unbracketed text represents a summary of the judgment.

Paragraph numbers of the judgment are bracketed.

[Bob Moles' comments on the judgment are contained in square brackets in bold type – he has made minor adjustments to some of the quotes from the judgment to clarify the point being made.]

The trial – forensic examination

Luminol is a 'screening test for blood' – it is not specific to blood and can produce false positives. [102]

[It is inaccurate to describe it as a 'test for blood'. Luminol will respond to over 100 different substances, including common cleaning agents, fish products (significant around

boats), paints and many others. It is inaccurate to describe the responses to the majority of materials as 'false positives' when they are known and acceptable responses to those materials – there is nothing 'false' about those responses. This means that Luminol tests results without an accompanying confirmatory test results should not be admitted in evidence in criminal trials – See *R v Keith Smart (Ruling no 1)* [2008] VSC 79 and the exclusion of Luminol test results – discussed in Moles research report on SNF case at p 5. Also the discussion of the IRA bombing cases in Sangha, Roach and Moles, *Forensic Investigations and Miscarriages of Justice*, Irwin Law, Toronto, 2010, chapter eight, Forensic Science Issues – "the judges referred to the conduct of the expert witnesses as 'analogous to fraud'. They had put forward the results of presumptive tests as if they were conclusive of the issues and had failed to properly articulate the reasoning processes involved". The overturning of the convictions in these cases caused such a scandal that they led to the establishment of the Criminal Cases Review Commission, described as one of the most significant reforms to the criminal process in British criminal history. There is no doubt that similar errors have occurred in the SNF case]

It luminesces if blood is present [102]

[This is inaccurate. Luminol contains inherent luminescent qualities, and will 'luminesce' if there is overspray - and no material to respond to. The witness said she sometimes used 'extra spray' for the photos]

The strength and nature of a reaction may indicate whether it is a true positive or false positive reaction. [102]

[The witness actually stated that she could determine whether the luminol was responding to blood or some other substance by 'the duration and quality of the glow and sparkle'. There is no scientific support for this proposition. If it were true luminol would no longer be a 'preliminary screening test' but a 'confirmatory test' – adding considerably to the value of the company which manufactures it. Objective specifications of 'duration' and 'quality' would need to be stated and recorded so that findings could be independently confirmed. Of course, none of that was done here.]

The other screening test used was the Hemastix test (HS) [103]

[Similar comments apply as above – noting that the HS test is a screening test and not a confirmatory test, so that the results obtained in this way should not be admitted in evidence without confirmatory test results as mentioned above]

The witness reported red/brown staining on steps to the wheel-house, at the entrance to the saloon, near the wheel, on the panel by the entrance and inside saloon, on cushions and bulkhead near seating and panel above it. Some were positive to HS and other 'numerous areas' were positive to luminol. [103]

There were numerous luminol positive areas on walkways, cabin roof, cockpit seat, floor, number of areas inside cockpit and near rope and winch. There were 8 areas on the deck and 3 in the cockpit which responded positively to luminol spray. [104]

[Not quite consistent with prior statement of 'numerous' responses in these areas, there was in fact just one area in the cockpit and one on the deck which gave a DNA profile linked to Bob Chappell.]

One luminol positive area on the deck gave a DNA profile of an unknown person (area 11) which was later matched to Meaghan Vass. [105]

The report said, 'Luminol positive area 11 (possible drops). Negative with HS Screening test for blood' [107]

The witness said "possible" drops means either a stain that is in the form of a drop or it was a drop from her spray bottle of luminol. [109]

[This is clearly unacceptable – the witness is saying that her report includes findings of 'possible' traces of 'blood' - which may amount to nothing more than the fact that she was dripping luminol from her spray bottle and when subjected to a further spray would luminesce and appear to be a positive response 'to blood'. This means she couldn't distinguish between findings 'of blood' and her contaminations of the potential crime-scene by her dripping of luminol at the scene. See Moles report on SNF appeal at p 20]

[I had completed a detailed report on the transcript of the trial in which I explained that the vast majority of McHoul's evidence on luminol and the test results for blood should not have been admitted at trial. It was in the IRA bombing cases in the UK where forensic scientists had used 'preliminary screening tests' (for nitro-glycerine) and informed the court that the results indicated that those tested had been involved in bomb-making. It was subsequently disclosed on appeal, some 20 years later, that common substances such as boot polish, nitrites in common soaps and the plastic backing on playing cards would each give similar positive results. When we published our book *Forensic Investigations*, Irwin Law Toronto, 2010, a Justice of the Canadian Supreme Court

referred to it in a prestigious lecture in Edinburgh stating that one of the achievements of the authors was that they had identified common causes of wrongful conviction in Australia, Britain and Canada. One of them was 'the use of preliminary tests as conclusive evidence'. Little were we to know at the time that the same mistake was about to be made in the SNF case in Hobart.

A copy of the above report was sent to the Director of the Forensic Science Service in Hobart in 2014. We were astonished to receive a response from the Asst. Police Commissioner which simply stated that she had confidence in the service being provided by FSST, and asked us not to correspond further about the matter. The Royal Commission reports in the cases of Splatt and Chamberlain had made it clear that forensic services in Australia should be 'operationally independent' of the police services. Knowing that, I was shocked to find that senior police officers in Tasmania were providing secretarial support to the Director of Forensic Services when asked to respond to matters on scientific issues.

The important point for present purposes is that The Director of FSST and Senior police officers in Tasmania were put on notice that the forensic evidence which had been given at the SNF trial was clearly incompetent, false and misleading and therefore should have been held to be inadmissible in legal proceedings. This means that in any further legal proceedings on these issues, they (and the prosecution acting on behalf of the Crown) had a duty to make appropriate disclosure of those errors <u>to the court</u>. Clearly that has not been done in this case. (As) this matter is to be the subject of an application for special leave to the High Court, one might expect that the prosecution

will inform <u>the court</u> that substantial inadmissible evidence had been admitted at trial]

The witness (McHoul) accepted that DNA processes cannot tell the age of a sample of blood. [111]

[This reference to McHoul discussing DNA should mention that she told the court at trial that she 'was not an expert on DNA'. She told the judge that she had overheard other people who were experts discussing DNA. The judge accepted that her 'overhearing experts' talking about it qualified her as an expert witness on the topic. This is clearly an unacceptable basis for the admission of 'expert' evidence – See Moles report on SNF trial at p 30]

Evidence of Jones on DNA

"If the tread of the shoe retaining a moist biological substance was to be acknowledged as the likely means of the transference, I believe it is reasonable to anticipate that at least one other similar stain resulting in the same DNA profile (or part thereof) would have been expected to have been deposited on the deck of 'Four Winds' as the person moved about the yacht. No such stain appeared to have been detected by Forensic Scientists … Therefore, **there is no evidence** to support the hypothesis that the DNA detected in sample 20 was the result of a secondary transfer event caused through foot traffic on the deck of 'Four Winds'." [165]

[This is the point I make later about footsteps as cause of secondary transfer resulting in similar but more substantial deposits every two paces]

The evidence of the DNA profile carried very real significance to the defence case… I accept that it could not have reasonably been expected of defence counsel to appreciate the potential significance of the electropherogram and to request that that primary source be provided. However, a general enquiry of FSST for more information about the profile would very likely have revealed the key information represented by the electropherogram. That information was available before the trial from FSST with the exercise of reasonable diligence. [209]

[This is not consistent with the statement of Kirby J in *Mallard*, that "there was no reason why the defence in a criminal trial should be obliged to 'fossick for information' of this kind and to which it was entitled. See Sangha, Roach, Moles, Forensic Investigations and Miscarriages of Justice, Irwin Law, Toronto, chapter five "Law on Miscarriages of Justice Australia" at p 162. He points out the risks of asking questions in cross-examination during a trial [or of an entity related to the police or prosecution as is the FSST as acknowledged by the judge on this appeal] See *Mallard v The Queen* [2005] HCA 68 at para 66. It is also clearly inconsistent with the requirements set out in the *Drummond* appeal and referred to by the judge in this appeal – "there is no obligation on an accused person to seek out information which the prosecution is obliged to produce"]

There may have been a tactical reason why this general probing and exploration of the DNA profile was not done. [210]

[The appeal judge is speculating that the defence counsel may have had some motive not to make inquiries. It may be that the reason was as explained by Kirby J – there are risks in making such inquiries.]

The report did not address the potential causal mechanism and possibilities such as contamination or secondary transfer. Meaghan

Vass's presence on the *Four Winds* was the obvious explanation and that was unassailed in the [expert's] report [at trial].

Another consideration may have been that the evidence could only be explored with FSST [Forensic Science Services Tasmania]. No other agency had the information. The strategy may have been not to seek additional information from FSST in case it brought to the prosecution's attention evidence unfavourable to the defence. [211]

[Clearly, the fact that the Forensic Services in Tasmania is a division of the police services limits its capacity to provide advice to the defence independently of police and prosecution services. Here the judge is acknowledging the risk to the defence to which we have referred].

These observations do not mean that the prosecution was absolved of its obligations in terms of disclosing evidence about the DNA profile, the relatively large quantity of DNA and also disclosing the opinion evidence of secondary transfer - before leading that evidence from Mr Grosser. These obligations remain significant in terms of assessing the position of the defence at the trial and warrant careful consideration. [211]

There was **no disclosure** of the opinion from Mr Grosser of secondary transfer as an explanation for the presence of the DNA. Mr Ellis was permitted to lead that evidence from Mr Grosser **without having provided a statement or proof of evidence.** The opinion was not foreshadowed and the defence had no warning of it. [212]

[This is a clear failure by the prosecution to act in accordance with the disclosure obligations set out in *Drummond* and referred to by the judge on this appeal. *Drummond* makes it clear that where the prosecution has failed to act in accordance

with its obligations, the discovery of that failure will constitute fresh evidence and will most likely also be compelling. The appeal judge here is acknowledging the failure, and whilst claiming to apply *Drummond* is acting contrary to it]

I accept that a relevant factor bearing on the question of reasonable diligence is **the lack of disclosure** of the opinion led from Mr Grosser regarding secondary transfer. This was relevant material and defence counsel were entitled to rely on the prosecutor's duty of disclosure here. [213]

Fairness dictates that a proof of evidence regarding this opinion should have been provided to the defence in reasonable time before he gave his evidence. It would have promoted an accurate understanding of Mr Grosser's opinion and assisted in identifying the limits of his opinion. The preparation of a proof may have led to the State disclosing other relevant evidence bearing on the same issue that had not been disclosed, such as the opinion advanced by Mr Grosser in his email to Detective Sinnitt that there was a relatively large amount of DNA in the sample. [214]

In assessing whether the defence exercised reasonable diligence - there was a clear invitation by the trial judge to defence counsel that he may request time to prepare his cross-examination – this would have enabled him to check the transcript of prosecution evidence, consult a forensic scientist – prepare cross-examination. [215]

[This is clearly inconsistent with Drummond - there is no obligation on an accused person to seek out information which the prosecution is obliged to produce]

The opportunity given by the learned trial judge to request time largely, if not completely, negated the unfairness in the

State not disclosing the opinion in advance by providing a proof. Perhaps there was a strategic advantage in defence counsel appearing to the jury to be unfazed by new evidence and being seen to proceed in a robust way. [216]

[It is shocking to suggest that defence counsel had some advantage by appearing calm in front of the jury whilst being ambushed. The situation was not dissimilar to that which occurred in Drummond. Peek J observed that 'defence counsel had only been told about the technical evidence which was to be led moments before the witness was called. Defence counsel's lack of understanding of the flaws in this evidence helped to explain why his final address to the jury on this topic would have taken 'less than a minute to say'. Drummond *(No 2)* [129]. Perhaps defence counsel in SNF 'appeared calm' because he didn't understand what the prosecution had but had not disclosed]

It is suggested that the opinion on secondary transfer was revealed towards the end of the trial. Given that the trial judge invited the defence to take time to prepare cross-examination, **the stage of the trial loses significance.** [217]

[So, a "late ambush" can be cured by the judge asking if defence would like to have time to think about it? The judge is suggesting that 'near the end of the trial', when defence counsel is made aware of the challenge to their position, he could have taken time to prepare cross-examination. So, defence counsel could have taken time to prepare a brief to an expert, identify an expert, inquire about the availability of the expert which may not be for some weeks ahead, wait for the expert to review the evidence and prepare a report, send it back to counsel who can then review it and prepare for further examination – all

in the closing stages of a trial? I think it would be polite to say that 'the stage of the trial' can never be 'without significance']

The expert evidence was not towards the end of the trial – it was a week before the trial finished – 29 Sept and 7 Oct - The complexity of the trial, a circumstantial case, the voluminous evidence, large number of witnesses, multiple factual issues are plain from the transcript and accepted. But **secondary transfer was a critical issue** for the defence and <u>there was an invitation to take time</u>.

[The emphasis here by the judge on the issue of due diligence by the defence is entirely misplaced. 'Due diligence' is said to be a component (although traditionally a minor and sometimes dispensable component) of fresh evidence. But Drummond makes it clear that where a non-disclosure by the Crown is involved, the issue of freshness is resolved by reference to the fact of the non-disclosure, rather than by a discussion of due diligence by the defence.

However, there is another approach to the issue of due diligence. The prosecution (or the appeal court) cannot raise a 'lack of freshness' argument against an appellant who has discovered errors in the case put forward by either the prosecution or an expert witness. The prosecution argument (or in this case, the appeal judge) presupposes that the appellant, by reasonable diligence, could have discovered the shortcoming at the time of the trial. Once the argument is raised by the prosecution, the response would be obvious. The appellant would ask the prosecution if *they* had exercised reasonable diligence at the time of the trial. A positive answer to that question would make it clear that the prosecution knew of the shortcomings at the time of the trial, but chose to conceal them, contrary to

their duty of disclosure. That discovery of the consciousness of wrongdoing by the Crown would then constitute the 'fresh evidence' required for the appeal to proceed. If the prosecution were to state that they had not exercised reasonable diligence at the time of the trial, then *that admission* would constitute the 'fresh evidence' of prosecutorial misconduct. It follows then that the prosecution (or the appeal court judge) cannot raise or act upon 'lack of freshness' in response to a claim of prosecutorial or expert witness error at trial.]

The other matter concerning disclosure is the failure to disclose before the trial and for the first part of the trial that there was a relatively large amount of DNA in the sample. [218]

Mr Grosser's evidence obliquely referred to, but did not adequately disclose, the fact that there was a relatively large amount of DNA in the sample. He discussed the mechanism of secondary transfer generally and a suggestion of a possibility of a large amount of DNA in this case. [219]

There was no evidence from an expert of a "significant amount of DNA"

He had knowledge of the quantity of DNA as a consequence of the disclosure of Mr Grosser's email to Detective Sinnitt, but that email was not part of the evidence before the jury.

The email was disclosed to counsel during the trial, the question is then, what opportunity was there for counsel to have adduced evidence with respect to the significance of the information it revealed? [220]

The disclosure of the email led to an application by defence counsel for Mr Grosser to be recalled. The application was opposed and refused. [221]

Defence counsel 'could have' cured defects

As soon as the email was disclosed, defence counsel could have made enquiries of an expert about the implications of the information disclosed such as the strong DNA profile and the relatively large amount of DNA - counsel could have sought the opinion of another scientist or considered speaking with Mr Grosser about its potential significance for secondary transfer as a possible explanation.

[After the application to recall Mr Grosser had already been refused?]

There would have been obvious difficulties for the appellant in presenting evidence on this appeal regarding these matters because senior counsel died in 2018. [223]

We know that a proof was not provided to the defence regarding secondary transfer, the evidence of secondary transfer was led without advance notice, and that defence counsel treated the email from Mr Grosser to Detective Sinnitt as having significance. If he had had knowledge of the strength of the DNA profile, it can be expected that he would have cross-examined Mr Grosser about it, which he did not do.

It is significant that there is no evidence suggesting that once Mr Grosser's email was disclosed there was anything preventing a forensic scientist from being <u>consulted</u>, <u>briefed</u> and, indeed, <u>called as a witness for the defence</u>. It seems there was that opportunity. [224]

[No problems doing all that whilst the trial is continuing?]

The email was disclosed on 30 September 2010, the balance of the State's case was presented over the ensuing days, the State closed its case on 7 October 2010.

Defence commenced its case on the same day

SNF's evidence concluded on 12 October and closing addresses commenced on 13 October After disclosure of the email there was time for the contents of it to be explored and evidence to be adduced.

Mr Grosser's evidence: the Director **took some liberties** with the evidence, or perhaps more precisely **with the absence of evidence**. I am not suggesting deliberately so. [240]

[Is it credible to suggest that a senior prosecutor could have taken such 'liberties' without 'deliberation'?]

I am not suggesting that the closing address was inconsistent with Mr Grosser's evidence.

[It clearly was]

The Director painted generalised scenarios which had not been explored in the evidence.

[In other words, he was speculating]

There had been no evidence that picking up a "trace" of DNA on a person's shoe could be transferred to a surface regardless of the viability of DNA from "anywhere" Ms Vass had been.

Timeframes, environmental factors, may impact on secondary transfer - whether the biological material was dry or wet, the variables on the adhering of biological substance to a shoe, contact with other surfaces while walking or getting into a car. Grosser's evidence was that as a general proposition secondary transfer was possible as a potential explanation but did not go into the variables.

The DPP strayed into 'conjecture'

The Director's scenario strayed away from the evidence into conjecture.

The misleading quality of the scenarios - it presented circumstances as giving rise to secondary transfer which had not been canvassed in the evidence and if they had been, would have been heavily qualified. It made it seem that any number of circumstances may feasibly give rise to secondary transfer when that had not been the subject of evidence. [241]

[This means the jury was misled – now come the excuses!]

This lack of evidence for generalised scenarios painted by the Director was apparent at the trial, and if the Director crossed the line

[why is the judge expressing this as a conditional proposition? It is clear that the prosecutor *did* cross the line.]

in terms of a prosecutor's duty, and in light of the "great trust" that jurors have in prosecution counsel, any unfairness, if it arose, **[again, the judge expresses this as a conditional proposition rather than an assertion that unfairness *had* occurred]**

could have been cured at the time of the trial or could have been the subject of the first appeal. [242]

[Surely the whole point of a second appeal is to deal with unfairness which has not been properly dealt with at trial or on a first appeal? Irrespective of whether the misrepresentations by the prosecutor 'could' have been cured at the trial, the fact is that they were not, unfairness had occurred, and the judge should determine whether it resulted in a substantial miscarriage of justice.

Counsel for the appellant could have asked the trial judge to remind [inform?] the jury that there was no evidence that the range of circumstances painted by Mr Ellis could lead to secondary transfer.

Why is the appeal judge putting this responsibility upon the defence counsel? Is it not the trial judge who has to ensure a fair trial? Why shouldn't the trial judge deal directly with a prosecutor who is misleading the jury on a crucial issue? The appeal judge is stating that *defence counsel* has the responsibility to ensure that the judge tells the jury that the prosecutor was misleading them? This is clearly contrary to *Drummond* which made it clear that defence counsel is entitled to rely upon the fact that the prosecutor will act in accordance with prosecutorial duties, and will not lead false or misleading evidence and, presumably, will not put false or misleading submissions to the jury.]

and further that all the jury had was evidence that it was possible that secondary transfer may occur by someone stepping in a biological substance and transferring it via the sole of their shoe. The first appeal did not assert any unfairness in the closing address.

[That is why we are having a second appeal]

It is important to bear in mind that <u>Mr Ellis's closing address was not the evidence</u>. The trial judge reminded the jury that their findings must be based on the evidence. [243]

[It is clearly possible, indeed quite likely, that the jury might have been misled into thinking that the DPP would not be so irresponsible as to propose something to them which did not have some evidential support? After a great deal of complex forensic evidence over many days, the jury might have been misled into thinking that the prosecutor was providing them with a summary of inferences which could be drawn from 'the evidence'. In effect, the prosecutor was opening up an

impermissible line of reasoning which could lead the jury into drawing inferences adverse to the accused on a central issue in the case. As was said in *GBF v The Queen* [2020] HCA 40 "the impugned statement allowed the jury to reason to guilt by an impermissible path". As in SNF, the appeal court in GBF reasoned that although the impugned statement should not have been made, there was no real possibility that the jury may have misunderstood earlier, correct directions of law that had been given, and no real possibility that the appellant had been deprived of a real chance of acquittal. Again, like SNF, the appeal court took into account the fact that neither the prosecutor nor defence counsel had applied for any redirection arising from the making of the impugned statement.

In *Azzopardi v The Queen* [2001] HCA 25 the court had stated that that the accused bore no burden, onus or obligation to prove anything – and as the impugned passage may have affected the jury's assessment of a critical witness … the appeal could not be dismissed under the proviso.

In *GBF*, the prosecution had argued that the impugned statement was 'a comment' which the jury may have found easier to ignore, and that the failure of counsel to seek a redirection meant that the integrity of the trial had not been compromised. The High Court pointed out that "any irregularity or failure to strictly comply with the rules of procedure and evidence is a miscarriage of justice" therefore, the invitation to the jury to engage in a false process of reasoning was an irregularity amounting to a miscarriage of justice.

The reasoning of the appeal court would appear to have repeated the errors of the appeal court in *GBF* and *Azzopardi*. It is clear from the following comments by the judge in SNF

that the reasons for avoiding the inevitable consequences of the prosecutorial submission are not acceptable, or in accordance with the principles laid down by the High Court.]

(Defence counsel) capably countered and contradicted the scathing references to Meaghan Vass's DNA as a red herring, and described the suggestion that DNA was "somehow trampled on board" as "pure fantasy". He described the efforts of the Director to try and suggest that her DNA got there by transference as a "desperation ploy". [244]

[This is to assume that the jury would accept the argument from defence counsel over that of the prosecutor.]

It would have been obvious to the jury that both closing addresses contained an element of hyperbole and conjecture. [245]

[This is to accept the DPP was putting 'hyperbole' and 'conjecture' to the jury in place of evidence or proper reasoning based upon admissible evidence. This is not the way in which serious criminal trials should be conducted.]

In assessing the impact of the scenario upon the jury, it is necessary to bear in mind the matters set out above, such as the strong counter to the Director's scenario in the defence closing, the trial judge's direction to the jury that closing addresses are not evidence and that the jury must base their findings on the evidence. It would have been evident to the jury that common to both addresses was a level of exaggeration and theatre. [247]

[The indications from *GBF* and *Azzopardi* would support the view that if the prosecutor engages in 'exaggeration and theatre' when addressing the jury, the effects of that cannot be offset by a general judicial direction, or a critique by defence counsel.]

If the evidence of Mr Jones [on this appeal] regarding the kind of circumstances required to give rise to the DNA profile had been before the jury, the Director would almost certainly not have painted that scenario or, if he had, it would have been, in its generalised terms, in conflict with Mr Jones's evidence. The suggestion that there need not be any close or direct connection between the receipt of the DNA "trace" on the person's shoe and the ultimate deposit on the boat could not have been made [by the DPP]. [248]

Before turning to whether the evidence of Mr Jones in this regard qualifies as substantial and highly probative – [249]

[How could there be any doubt after what has just been said?]

The evidence of Mr Jones regarding rarity of an occurrence of secondary transfer is a 'relative concept' and this perspective of relative rarity only takes the jury so far and it doesn't exclude the specific circumstances which may face the jury. [250]

[This is a repetition of the "Bromley approach" which de-valued or undermined the significance of the overwhelming expert evidence which was presented on the appeal. The judges there said the principles and conclusions of the experts were expressed in 'general terms' and therefore the specific factors of the witnesses' evidence might lead to different conclusions. This is a bit like saying that legal principles or rules are expressed in general terms, so may not apply to specific circumstances of an individual case. Philosophically this is profoundly unsound as all human knowledge is expressed at varying levels of 'generality'. The clear guidance of the experts in Bromley (and SNF) was developed with the circumstances of those cases in mind. The judges are trying to avoid the necessary implications of that advice by suggesting that the

'particularities' are at variance with that advice when that is plainly not so. We should cry 'foul'!]

[252] **[this para engages in the devaluing exercise to trivialise the impact of the expert evidence by asserting that 'not finding' other traces does not mean they were not there – rather like the medical board in Keogh – 'the absence of evidence is not evidence of absence'! The key point is that material on a foot would be deposited every 'two feet' so it would not be hard to find? Two paces from the deposit in the direction of travel – if it arrived 'by foot' – there would be another and larger deposit – given that with each step the quantity for distribution would be diminished. This would continue every two paces, with increasing quantities, until one arrived at the initial deposit, or at the place where the traveller arrived by vehicle. The inability to find such further deposits supports the hypothesis that the deposit did not arrive as a result of foot travel. In other words, the failure to find additional deposits *falsifies* the hypothesis that it arrived as a result of foot travel. Given the constant references to the 'sensitivity' of the various testing methods, it would be unlikely that there had been some process by which all traces of such deposits had been removed.]**

Summary of key errors identified:

- Judge failed to recognise that luminol test was inadmissible forensic evidence
- That this was incompetent, false and misleading evidence was not disclosed at the appeal by the prosecution

- Failure to recognise that some DNA evidence was incomplete & misleading
- Excusing that the Director 'strayed into conjecture' about secondary transfer of DNA
- Judge's misplaced emphasis on due diligence by the defence, actually a requisite by prosecution
- Judge excusing impermissible prosecutorial speculation as 'liberties' & 'hyperbole' & 'exaggeration and theatre'

Keep Vass off the boat!

Those in the legal establishment with an interest in protecting the conviction wanted to keep Meaghan Vass 'off the boat', metaphorically speaking, because her eye witness testimony of Bob Chappell's fight on board *Four Winds* contradicts the prosecution's case against Sue Neill-Fraser. But the Crown failed to explain why a terrified young woman would willingly put herself through emotional hell for years and put herself potentially in harm's way?

From Sue Neill-Fraser's murder trial in 2010 right up till the appeal judges retired (on March 3, 2021) to consider their verdicts, both the former and current DPPs, plus TasPol, as well as a handful of zealous 'convictioners', appear determined to keep Meaghan Vass off the *Four Winds* – and to undermine her credibility.

Yet no-one has put forward a reasonable alternative narrative to the one they want to dismiss that is consistent with the Vass admissions. If she wasn't on board when the crime was committed, what narrative could explain her actions and the facts?

An alternative narrative

- has to fit the timeline of events;
- has to include her DNA being found on the deck;
- has to explain her convincing confession on *60 Minutes*;
- has to explain her matching testimony on day 1 of the appeal and her sworn statement to the same effect;
- has to be set in the context of a strong & credible motive, supported by evidence.

As long as Vass could be 'kept off the boat', so to speak, the Crown's circumstantial case might be upheld (or justified), even though it lacks any primary evidence and is pure speculation. Just read the many newspaper articles, the three books (and this ,the fourth), several TV programs, a documentary film (Shadow of Doubt) and a 6-part documentary TV series, *Undercurrent* and the 29-epsiode podcast, *Who Killed Bob?* which all examine the case - and find it a miscarriage of justice. Or check the barristers, lawyers and legal academics who challenge, with respect of course, the conviction.

Even without Meaghan Vass, the prosecution doesn't have a credible case against Sue Neill-Fraser. As the late, acclaimed Chester Porter KC put it - on camera - in November 2013, "it would not be at all surprising if the jury had acquitted this lady because the evidence was so weak against her..." But evidently the jury did not entertain a reasonable doubt ... we'll never know why not.

The blustery conditions on Australian Day 2009 bounced the moored yachts up and down. A young landlubber like Meaghan Vass, possibly affected by drugs and /or alcohol, not to mention her witnessing the bloody fight between Bob and the men with

Vass, would be highly likely to be seasick. She told 60 Minutes she vomited on the deck, which provided her DNA. (See transcript of *60 Minutes* interview page 55.) One would say that scenario is more credible than the propositions put by both DPPs (Ellis at trial as well as at the first seeking leave to appeal to the High Court, and Coates at the second appeal) that Vass was not likely to have made the DNA deposit herself but it was a secondary transfer, OR she made it at a later time, when boarding the yacht in dry dock ... The desperation to keep Vass off the boat on January 26 led them to propose alternatives that contradict each other. The truth doesn't tolerate contradictions.

The DNA in perspective

From the moment at trial when then DPP Tim Ellis SC branded Meaghan Vass' DNA deposit as a 'red herring', the Crown's case deflected attention from the absence of evidence against the accused to an argument over the DNA. This DNA was not from either the accused, Neill-Fraser, or the assumed victim, Bob Chappell. It was at the crime scene, but it was not a result of the crime alleged by the Crown.

It was a big red alarm bell, though, for the Crown's case. At the time, the prosecution had no idea what Meaghan Vass would or could say about being at the crime scene – but whatever it was would seriously, perhaps fatally, damage the Crown case, because the Crown KNEW it had no evidence that would convince the jury beyond reasonable doubt. The Crown KNEW that an eye witness could vaporise the charge of murder against Sue Neill-Fraser. The Crown KNEW it didn't really have a case. The Crown couldn't even place the accused at the crime scene at the relevant time....as the relevant time was not known.

Both Vass the witness and her DNA sample had to be discredited, destroyed, defused... The objective, after all, was to win a conviction. In the absence of a body and a weapon, that could be done only if the jury heard how the accused killed the victim. The Crown obliged ....

Students of the case in the future will wonder how the convulsed tussle about that DNA sample infected the fair trial and subsequent appeals. How could its dismissal or its denigration prove Sue Neill-Fraser guilty of murder beyond reasonable doubt?

Years later, when Vass finally told the world on *60 Minutes* what she had seen on *Four Winds* that day, the Crown's fears were vindicated.

Tasmania's vertically integrated legal establishment has refused to deal with the facts that led to what we say is a wrongful conviction. Stubbornly, because since Meaghan Vass gave her extensive, heart wrenching interview to Liam Bartlett on *60 Minutes* that aired on March 10, 2019, effectively the whole world could now see that Sue Neill-Fraser should not have been convicted for a murder she did not commit; an eye witness had destroyed the Crown's false narrative.

In this case, the Crown could never be accused of behaving like the model litigant it is supposed to be, but when the pressure intensified with the *60 Minutes* interview (even though it wasn't broadcast live on Ch 9 in Tasmania, it was quickly found online), the mantra to '*keep Vass off the boat*' also intensified.

How they (protectors of the conviction) tried to 'keep Vass off the boat' - examples:

- At trial, dismiss her DNA on the deck of *Four Winds* as a 'red herring', a secondary transfer, probably on someone's shoe

(also accepted at the first appeal in 2011 and also at seeking leave to appeal to the High Court in 2012)

- Police issue a statement after the *60 Minutes* program in March 2019 that police had interviewed her and she had changed her story from the one she had just told on *60 Minutes*, implying she was not on board; not true, but Integrity Commission dismisses complaint;
- The take-your-pick submissions of the DPP at the March 2021 appeal were that:-
  1) Meaghan Vass was not on board; her DNA was a secondary transfer; no reference to vomit
  2) her DNA was detected in a swab recorded on January 30 when *Four Winds* was at the Goodwood facility; so Vass was not on board on January 27 - because her DNA would not have lasted in usable form more than 2 days on the deck, if she deposited it on January 27 (unsupported forensic conclusion, yet in this scenario, the prosecution accepts the deposit as primary, contrary to above); no reference to vomit
  3) perhaps she sneaked on board, maybe on January 28 after the boat was placed at the Cleanlift facility (no evidence, no CCTV footage) - in this scenario, too, the deposit is accepted as primary; no reference to vomit.

"CORRECT THIS INJUSTICE, THE PRODUCT OF OUR TASMANIAN LEGAL FAMILY"

The High Court shut the door on Sue Neill-Fraser's case on August 12, 2022 by refusing her leave to appeal (for the second time). But it couldn't shut down the clamour of her many supporters who still believed it to be a terrible injustice. Irked by all the ongoing criticisms and complaints, Simon Gates, the then President of the Tasmanian Law Society, a well meaning, handsome young man, sprang to the defence of the legal establishment and penned a letter to the editor for the Hobart Mercury. It backfired.

Prior to being called to the Bar in 2021, Simon was a Partner at McLean, McKenzie and Topfer, Barristers and Solicitors, for four years, where he had worked since 2013, specialising in workers compensation, personal injuries and administrative law.

Before entering private legal practice in 2013, Simon held the position of Senior Legal Advisor (2012-13) and Legal Advisor (2011) to the Tasmanian State Attorney-General and Crown Counsel in the Office of the Solicitor-General for the State of Tasmania between 2007 and 2011.

Criminal law had never been his speciality. But clearly, he means well. In 2005 and 2006, prior to admission to legal practice, Simon lived and worked in Timor-Leste, working primarily as an Australian Volunteers International funded legal and policy advisor in the minerals, oil and gas sector for the Timor-Leste Government.

Gates' letter appeared across the top of two pages as the day's Talking Point in the Mercury's opinion pages on August 23, 2022, a couple of weeks after the High Court decision. The big, bold headline across the two pages read **"Neill-Fraser's supporters risk undermining confidence in legal system"** It was subheaded: **"Sustained criticism of our criminal justice system over the handling of the Susan Neill-Fraser case is unhelpful and a waste of money, writes Simon Gates"**

The Gates letter:

On August 12th, 2022, the High Court of Australia rejected Susan Neill-Fraser's application for special leave to appeal the Tasmanian Court of Criminal Appeals' decision not to allow a retrial.

As a general rule, the Law Society does not comment on individual cases. However, where sustained criticism of the judiciary, the prosecution, and the police investigation risks undermining public confidence in our criminal justice system, as has occurred in this case, the Law Society feels compelled to comment.

Ms. Neill-Fraser's case or aspects of it have now been considered by five high court judges, eight Tasmanian Supreme Court judges, and 12 of Ms. Neill-Fraser's peers comprising the jury at the original trial. Those 12 jurors considered all of the evidence adduced at the trial and each were satisfied beyond reasonable doubt that Ms. Neill-Fraser's guilt was the only rational conclusion which was open on the whole of the evidence that they accepted as jurors.

New legislation was also enacted by Parliament which allowed Ms. Neill-Fraser further opportunity to put fresh and compelling evidence before the Supreme Court and to seek a retrial. Ms. Neill-Fraser availed herself of that legislation and appealed to the Court of Criminal Appeal. That appeal was dismissed by a majority of two out of three judges. Notably, during the appeal hearing, Ms. Neill-Fraser's own barrister informed the court that Ms. Neill-Fraser no longer sought to rely on the evidence of Ms. Meghan Vass given during that hearing, conceding that it would not help Ms. Neill-Fraser's case. It is vital that those commenting on the case consider the evidence as a whole as the jury did, and not just small aspects of it. This will help ensure that any criticism of the case and the criminal justice system is made from an informed position.

A summary of the evidence is contained in Justice Wood's judgment in the 2021 Court of Criminal Appeal decision and the March 6th, 2012 Court of Criminal Appeal decision, which is also publicly available on AustLII Ed Au. Much of the evidence considered by the jury has seldom if ever been mentioned in recent public commentary on the case. One of the errors that is often made by those commenting on the case is to assume that if doubt can be cast on one or more pieces of evidence that therefore means that there has been injustice.

However, as the trial judge told the jury on October 14th, 2010, the commission of a crime may be proved beyond reasonable doubt by circumstantial evidence provided that, A, all the facts and circumstances from which the conclusion of guilt is drawn must be established to the satisfaction of the jury, and, B, the jury must be satisfied beyond reasonable doubt that the conclusion of guilt is the only rational conclusion which is open on the whole of the evidence that the jury accepts.

The jury found that, based on the evidence as a whole, there was no rational hypothesis consistent with Ms. Neill-Fraser's innocence. It is not enough that people speculate about other possible theories or explanations. Any such hypotheses must be considered in the context of the evidence as a whole. I note the call by Ms. Neill-Fraser's supporters for a Commission of Inquiry.

I strongly urge anyone considering supporting such a call to consider all of the evidence presented at the trial and of the history of this case before the courts. The millions of dollars that would be spent on a Commission of Inquiry into this case could be spent bolstering Tasmania's insufficient legal aid budget and ensuring that all Tasmanians have access to adequate legal representation when they encounter the justice system.

Does Gates think that people were just whingeing without good reason - for over a decade? Gates seems unaware that those critical of the handling of this case include several barristers and lawyers who have indeed considered all of the evidence, that many of the criticisms raised involve prejudicial behaviour in court. His comments appear naïve, uninformed or plain incorrect. Unwise, too, is his trying to protect the conviction by citing the number of judges who have considered the case – or parts of it. For one thing, including five High Court judges is especially embarrassing for any lawyer and especially for someone of Gates' stature; the High Court judges (only three) refused leave to hear the appeal. That hardly constitutes consideration of the case. For another, there have been detailed and legally supported critiques of all the appeal judges' decisions, and of the trial judge.

To say that the comment backfired would be an understatement. Unsurprisingly, seeing how it revealed Gates' limited grasp of the case in all its complexities, his Talking Point attracted derision from supporters and motivated recently retired Hobart prosecutor Tony Jacobs, to join the many critics with an extensive analysis that was sent to the Tasmanian Law Society a month later.

Over in his West Hobart white picket fence home, Jacobs read Gates' letter in the Mercury with growing unease and set about the mammoth task of reviewing the case in detail. And when he did, he felt a moral obligation to speak up. The result is as close as Tasmania seems likely to get to an independent review of the matter - by a local lawyer no less – who is versed in the criminal law who has no agenda other than to protect the legal system and no connection to the case. The same ambition as Gates, but with the benefit of experience in criminal law.

In his extensively detailed, tightly spaced 10-page letter of September 27, 2022, to the Law Society's Executive Director, Luke Rheinberger, responding to the Gates article, Jacobs pleads: "Savagely scrutinise my words, but if you cannot fault them, please speak up to help correct this injustice, the product of our Tasmanian legal family." The Law Society did not respond.

Jacobs reveals "serious matters never before raised," which "show that her conviction in October 2010 should have been immediately overturned." Those serious matters are critical of the legal fraternity and include:

- A misstatement of scientific fact made by the trial Judge on a very serious & pertinent issue toward the conclusion of his Summing Up to the Jury,
- "flagrant incompetence" of defence counsel, the late David Gunson,
- the failure of the solicitors lodging her 2011 appeal to raise these issues,
- the failure of the solicitor lodging her 2012 High Court appeal (Madeleine Ogilvie, now Minister for Small Business & Racing)
- and "the failure of the Tasmanian Appeal Court in 2012 to, of its own motion, raise these issues."

Jacobs, pointing out that he concentrated on the legal issues, begins by listing his research: "I have done what Simon requests. Read all 1550 pages of the trial transcript. Read the decision of the 2012 Appeal Court. Read the 18 page in total 7/9/2012 High Court hearing and decision. Read Mr Justice Brett's decision. Read the total 544 paragraph November 2021 decision and other materials. Quite a few of these I've read more than once. Simon said that the jury found that based on the evidence as a whole, there was no rational hypothesis consistent with innocence. But that verdict was based on what they heard and were told."

Jacobs goes on to provide extensive instances of incompetence by Gunson, and includes examples of appeal judge Justice Wood making excuses for Gunson's inaction on several occasions.

"Mr Gunson was apparently both Solicitor & Counsel; not unusual in Tasmania. I don't point to just one action or inaction, but to the combined effect of many. Some of these were clear after the trial in 2010, others became clear after the 2021Appeal decision, particularly in the decision of Wood J which outlines much of the available evidence. Jacobs concludes, "I suggest he (Gunson) was simply out of his depth".

There is criticism, too, of the trial judge, Blow (now CJ) "for telling the jury just after lunch near the end of a lengthy Summing Up that Ms Vass might have urinated somewhere in Hobart, and a Police Officer walked on it and then walked it onto the boat whereas the scientific fact is that urine has very little DNA & what it does have, dissipates quickly." (see above)

Notable by its absence from the Jacobs review is any critical mention of DPP Tim Ellis putting his murder scenario speculation to the jury. When asked about this, Jacobs agrees he should have included reference to that.

(- - But in a conversation for this book, Jacobs refers to how, soon after the appointment of Jack Johnston as Tasmanian Police Commissioner, Johnston was arrested and strip-searched before facing court for the first time in October 2008, after standing himself aside in August that year during the investigation.

Johnston pleaded not guilty in October 2008 to two charges of disclosing official secrets to the State Government. It was alleged that in April 2008, just weeks after his appointment, Johnston gave details of an ongoing police investigation into corruption allegations against government MPs to then police minister Jim Cox and then premier Paul Lennon.

It was alleged the MPs being investigated would have benefited in their defence against the corruption claims with Mr Johnston's information.

"Ellis prosecuted Johnston before Evans J (it was not under the Criminal Code, so no jury). The judge dismissed the Ellis

claims pretty quickly. Ellis then publicly criticised the fact that he could not appeal the decision which he claimed was wrong," recalls Jacobs.

There were ultimately no charges of corruption against the MPs concerned, wrote Paul Carter in news.com.au. "Johnston was cleared to return to work after the state's Director of Public Prosecutions exhausted his final legal bid to have the top cop face criminal charges. The High Court in Melbourne rejected DPP Tim Ellis's application for leave to appeal a permanent stay on the proceedings made by Tasmanian Supreme Court Justice Peter Evans in August."

Jacobs recalls how "Tim seemed to go off on a tangent about this when few could see any wrong. He was making explosive statements. When Johnston was charged by Ellis and forced to stand aside, then Premier David Bartlett announced that the recent retired Commissioner Richard McCreadie was temporarily returning. Ellis criticised this and said that McCreadie also might be charged. It left the Premier and McCreadie very embarrassed and the Deputy Commissioner then started acting as Commissioner. I was surprised that the Premier didn't tell Ellis to keep out of the Government's business."

But what Jacobs did include in his letter were four significant issues not disclosed, "for the simple reason that Mr Ellis did not know about them," he states.

"The first is the evidence re the electropherogram. (**see A below**) This was surely major evidence which apart from anything else destroyed Mr Ellis's strong claims of someone walking the deposit and of anything else being a red herring.

The second is the evidence about the, apparently, false Mt Nelson address and it's pinpointing of that day.

The third is the evidence re Ms Vass (possibly hanging around Goodwood).

The fourth is the fact that Mr Grosser, in a conversation with Detective Sinnitt, had given details that suggested that (DNA source) E20, was unlikely a walked on sample. Mr Gunson did get part of this evidence before the court through cross examination of the detective. But the jury never heard all the known second or third above evidence, nor, of course, the electropherogram evidence.

These failings surely constituted a mistrial."

A "Not taking the opportunity to accept the standard offer, twice made in FSST (Forensic Science Services Tasmania) reports, to visit by arrangement & discuss with scientists. The words used included "full notes (including photos) & details of test methods & results of examinations & tests are available to Defence Counsel...FSST provides an impartial service & Defence counsel are encouraged..."

"Normally Defence Counsel do not take up this offer but here we had a wholly circumstantial murder trial where suddenly in March 2010 a DNA sample is matched to someone & that someone is refusing to speak to Police or make a statement.

"And, where there are 3 unmatched male DNA samples.

"The scientists had given evidence at preliminary proceedings but Mr Gunson had not explored such issues. Mr Max Jones, a Victorian Forensic Scientist did visit FSST in 2014 & found the very strong evidence that was there for Mr Gunson in 2010 - that there was an electropherogram of area 20 (the Vass DNA) which showed "an unambiguous single source"..."no significant evidence of stochastic variation," high "allele peak heights" & "molecular weight loci."

"And, that this was "strongly inconsistent" with a "touch" scenario.

"This was the alleged "fresh" evidence in the 2021Appeal. Wood J reviewed it (paras 196-203), said that this possibly very significant evidence should have been disclosed but Held that it was not fresh evidence because Mr Gunson could with reasonable diligence have discovered & adduced it.

And, during the trial, Mr Gunson could have requested a visit, particularly pertinent after undisclosed opinions of Mr Grosser had come out in cross examination of Detective Sinnitt."

Critical of Gunson's examination of Vass, he criticizes Gunson for "Not questioning the alleged details of the alleged stealing that led to her arrest & the DNA sample. Was she alone? Was it from a shop/ from a residence/from a vehicle/ from a boat?"

Later, Jacobs asks rhetorically about solicitors in the 2011 appeal: "Why didn't they raise Mr Gunson's incompetence and the stark failures of prosecutorial disclosure obligations?"

Simon Gates made the point that so many judges had been involved; "Fair enough," comments Jacobs, "but I suggest that Mrs Neill-Fraser was met with a Catch 22 situation whichever way she turned after the trial."

Jacobs says near the end of his letter that "obviously with my background (*as former prosecutor*) I have an interest. "I would have been very happy to find that all was just and above board. It clearly was not and is not. I feel that I have a strong moral obligation to speak up."

The Simon Gates letter was published on August 23, 2022; Tony Jacobs' review was sent to the Law Society on September 27, 2022. He received a reply in January, 2023.

Confident in his analysis, Jacobs made a brief speech at the seminar titled *Lifting the Lid on Miscarriages of Justice,* held at Hobart's Old Woolstore, on 24 November, 2022, in which he offered a reward of $10,000 to any lawyer who proved his analysis wrong. It has not been claimed.

An imposing man with bushy white eyebrows, Jacobs leads me into his card room, where he and his card group have played every week for 50 years. A drinks cabinet stands against the wall opposite the window. A kitten and a puppy play near the front door. With Ukraine very much in the news, and his wife being from Ukraine, before we turn to the matter at hand, he reveals how he was able to bring his daughter and her young Ukrainian family to Australia from Warsaw (after their fleeing Ukraine), using all his frequent flyer points.

Jacobs' analysis is not some pop-up intervention; he has followed the case for a decade. But his intervention seems to have shamed his legal fraternity into silence. He has spoken to several colleagues who share his disagreement with the conviction, but do not wish to 'go public' with their view. Jacob shrugs; it's Tasmania, a conservative people who trust their institutions. "And some of the lawyers seem to worry about how judges might react to them…but that fear is unfounded," he says. In the early days, in a casual conversation, even the DPP's junior, Jack Shapiro, had expressed some reservations about the strength of the prosecution case. Judging by his subsequent prosecutorial fervour, Shapiro clearly overcame his reservations.

In conclusion, Jacobs makes the point that Neill-Fraser being paroled "should not alter the need for a thorough enquiry, at least into the above legal aspects."

In later correspondence mid-2023, Jacobs provided this author with further material and comments, including what he calls "The vital letter from Mara House. It was a Colony 47 residence for ladies under 21 & is in New Town (about 3 km from Hobart CBD) & 5 K's from the Northern suburb Police boat compound. You'll recall that Tim Ellis & the Judge made much of Ms Vass "homeless in the Northern suburbs". She wasn't at that time.

The letter, from Mara House Manager Shari Collis on 23/3/2010 to Sgt Shane Sinnitt, "shows the vital info that Police (Snr Const Robin Button, a part time detective in the Kingston area S of Hobart) knew of a burglary by Ms Vass with others 2 days after the homicide on the boat.

"Also names 3 males Police should have tested for DNA. Sam Devine is, of course, named by some as the killer.

"This letter was part of Sgt Sinnitt's records photo stated by Gunson 1/2 way thru the trial. It & all 100+ other pages were tendered de bene esse before Brett J in 2018. I don't know if anybody else read this but they CERTAINLY SHOULD HAVE. It's input would have dramatically changed the trial & Appeals. I didn't get this until January."

"Mara House documentation re: Meaghan Vass 26/1 - 30/1/2009
Sorry but time of Meaghans return from sleepover at Heath's place on 25/1 not recorded.

26/1/09 Meaghan requested a sleepover at Sam's place 8/7 Onslow Place Mt Nelson as worker had said no to another sleepover at Heath's as **she** had **returned** to the service with a hangover.

Left the service at 3.50pm on 26/1 and was to call the service with Sam's phone number so worker could verify where she was before sleepover was actioned. Had not returned to the service by 5.40 and was breaching curfew, and was not answering her phone.

26/1. Night shift worker tried to contact Meaghan again, no answer.

27/1. No time documented. But a day shift entry 9 - 3.30 pm. Entry says MV self exiting, going to Annie Kenney.

27/1. No time documented. But afternoon shift entry. 3 - 8pm. Entry says MV back and Informed of being grounded on Fri and Sat night for going on a sleepover without consent.

27/1. Sleepover form for Sam's at Onslow place.

28/1. Did not return by 5pm curfew. Afternoon shift.

28/1. Did not return, mum and police contacted (as per MH Policy)

29.1 Returned to the service at 4.50pm (with another resident) Stated she was going back out for the night as she had plans. Worker informed her she was putting her accommodation at risk if she left. MV left the service at 6.40pm and stated she did not care about the consequences of leaving.

29/1. Meaghan informed that if she left the service she would be exited.

29/1. Phone call to MV mum re: MV leaving the service. Mother stated a friend of hers (police officer) informed her that and another resident were involved in a break and enter the evening before. Mother stated that MV and the other resident were with a man named Matt.

MV did not return to the service after she left on 29/1. File closed. There is nothing in our records that documents any injury."

In correspondence with the Tasmanian Bar Association in March 2023 (to which he received no reply), he sets out his "16 Grounds of Negligence and it ends showing how very simply Gunson could have got her acquitted.," including references to the Mara House letter.

These are his 16 grounds:

"PARTICULARS OF Mr GUNSON's FLAGRANT INCOMPETENCE

1. Not ensuring Mara House (Colony 47, 19 Forster St), accommodation records before jury.
2. Not ensuring evidence in of Vass break & enter on 28th Jan (S/Const Robyn Button).
3. Not asking Sgt Sinnitt as to 3 names in Mara letter & re Police record of Jan 28th crime.

4. Not asking Vass as to Court companions/friends/associates. She had 2 "very rough looking" male companions according to DPP personnel.
5. Not exploring with Police re DNA of the 3 +2 men above c.f. 3 untraced DNA deposits on yacht & not asking as to those men's records with Police.
6. Not visit FSST & speak to scientists including Carl Grosser. Was twice invited by the usual letter. Electropherogram 260 x 210 mm. should been tendered.
7. Failing to establish from scientists that "very unlikely that the DNA (sample) was walked on." [Was in Grosser e-mail in Sgt Sinnitt's records+ personal query would have disclosed]
8. Not object to hearsay in re-examination of Sinnitt- 'Vass said believed may been hanging around Goodwood area'
9. In X-Ex of only 2 minutes being nasty to Vass on irrelevant issue ("pretty sure" then living @ Annie Kenny c.f@ Stainforth Court in Basha evidence)-leading to violent attack by Ellis-to jury, Tas Appeal & High Court [& given as excuse not to recall Ms Vass]
10. Ellis having savaged this (p.1407-8) = possible jury intense dislike-no apology/ not make clear to jury that might be his fault but was not N-F's fault.
11. Not refer to McHoul evidence= 26 x 21cm (10.25 x 8.25inch) [did say "significant amount"]
12. Not refer to Mrs Sanchez' evidence (Bob Chappel's sister & was then staying with them, as often did). She said that they "seemed supportive & devoted."
13. Not calling family/friends re close/loving relationship [later claimed on tv],

14. Not refer to sadness/stress@ loss partner/culprit not caught. We act different under stress.
15. Not asking Judge to recall jury & correct his urine-DNA suggestion (had 24 hours to do so).
16. Agreeing jury should not view the yacht [I don't pretend to know all the details]

"In the traditional manner Mr Ellis would have called Mara Manager & Sgt Button upon request & he probably would then have wanted Ms Vass recalled to try & explain.

If Gunson had been very smart, he could have said nothing & himself called the Mara Manager & Const Button, leaving, I strongly believe, huge doubts & a very embarrassed Tim Ellis.

The core Tas Appeal point & the only High Court one was the failure of the Judge to himself recall Ms Vass [the Prosecutor could not be forced to] but that would only have been as to the address error. (Gunson could re-called Ms Vass himself if vital-probably would needed Court help to get her there). The Attorney General has claimed "Tasmania & Australia's highest Courts have considered (the case) in great detail." The simple fact is that the total High Court transcript including decision, is only 18 pages & that neither the Tasmanian or the High Court Appeals raised the issue of Mr Gunson's flagrant incompetence or the serious misstatement of fact by His Honour.

I suggest that they on top of the Prosecution disclosure failures would have almost certainly resulted in the conviction being overturned.

To have done so would have likely brought the Appeal lawyer (s) a lifetime enemy in Mr Gunson but I assume that the reason is just that all the transcript & all the documents were not scrutinized.

If an Australian had been so treated overseas, I believe the justice failures would be a matter of concern raised in Canberra. But what about injustice in our Tasmania in the 21st Century?

I invite you & your Committee members to scrutinize thoroughly what I've said. I will be delighted if you can show that I'm wrong. But if you accept that I am correct I ask that you honour our profession by publicly supporting me. I look forward to your considered opinions."

At the time of writing (June 2023) Jacobs has not had a response to this letter of March 2023 from the Tasmanian Bar Association.

But even before his September letter to the Law Society, Jacobs had written to Attorney-General Elise Archer in January, 2022, suggesting an 'Enquiry Panel' comprising three retired mainland judges. Archer claimed impotence as the matter was then still before the courts. Jacobs wrote to her again in September with a copy of his submission. In October, Archer replied, predictably enough, claiming that highest courts had considered the case in great detail. (Jacobs pointed out that her claim was incorrect; the High Court did not consider the case at all, never mind 'in great detail'.)

No Attorney-General across their portfolio could fail to know enough of this controversial case to understand that, as Michael Gaffney's adjournment speech on November 15, 2022, to the Legislative Council pointed out, "the courts are only ever as good as the evidence put before them and the appeal courts are only ever as good as the points of appeal put to them, and vulnerable witnesses are only as good as the protection and support provided to them. When the system fails, or more to the point, when lawyers fail, miscarriages of justice can occur and it is up to the First Law Officer of the Land to recognise these failures and address them."

Gaffney MLC (Independent, Mersey), tabling Jacobs' critique of the case, also turned her own words back on Archer, when she pleaded that the courts' decisions be respected or risk undermining the rule of law and the judiciary. "To be deliberately blind to [those failures] is what will undermine confidence in the legal system," he says accusingly. The legal system in Tasmania doesn't seem to need anyone to undermine confidence ... it has done that adequately by itself.

Gaffney also revealed that "Robert Richter KC and David Edwardson (Jeff Thompson's lawyer in the prison surveillance device matter), wrote to the Attorney-General in early November 2022, a detailed letter also calling for a Commission of Inquiry. There has been no response.

"Mr President," added Gaffney in conclusion, "I call upon the Attorney-General to establish a Commission of Inquiry into the Sue Neill-Fraser conviction and wider systemic entrenched issues in our justice system which may have led to other miscarriages of justice in Tasmania too."

ANATOMY OF A WRONGFUL CONVICTION

The Sue Neill-Fraser case and its flagrant errors. None of the matters summarised below (from previous chapters) have been considered by any appeal court.

Identified by Flinders University legal academic Dr Bob Moles:

- Luminol test results are not admissible
- Luminol test results in photograph in the dinghy are seriously prejudicial
- Pathology evidence inadmissible
- Submissions by prosecutor and judge inadmissible
- Jury misinformed concerning drug smuggling operations
- Judge – circumstantial case wrongful summing up to jury

Identified by former prosecutor Tony Jacobs

- flagrant incompetence by defence counsel, the late David Gunson (see above),
- the failure of the solicitors lodging her 2011 appeal to raise these issues,
- the failure of the solicitor lodging her 2012 High Court appeal
- the failure of the Tasmanian Appeal Court in 2012 to, of its own motion, raise these issues.

- Evidence not disclosed re electropherogram (of Vass DNA), destroying prosecutor's claim of transferred deposit;
- Evidence not disclosed about the false Mt Nelson address (given by Vass);
- Failure to object to inadmissible hearsay evidence from Detective Sinnitt re Vass possibly hanging around Goodwood;
- Evidence not disclosed that Mr Gosser in conversation with Detective Sinnitt re DNA unlikely to have been walked on

The Etter Selby papers & the police investigation

The August 2021 Etter Selby investigation report states that: "This paper explores significant police shortcomings in the investigation, along with their failure to disclose key evidence to the Crown in the Sue Neill-Fraser case. It brings to light information that has **not been presented to the court** at any stage of the initial trial, subsequent appeals nor the latest appeal [then] before the Supreme Court of Tasmania.

THE (EVER-ACTIVE) SUE NEILL-FRASER SUPPORT GROUP

As if fate were timing events for dramatic effect, the Sue Neill-Fraser Support Group's sombre email to its 100 signed up members on August 12, 2022, that the High Court had refused leave for her appeal was soon followed by their elated email on September 16, 2022, that Sue had been granted parole. The Support Group had kept its members – and the media – informed of every step in the tortuous route of the case for well over a decade.

The dedicated Support Group Inc. have been active since even before her controversial murder conviction in October 2010. Who are they? What drives them? How did they coalesce into the determined and persistent citizen army they have remained? What have they achieved? (Apart from their Lynn Giddings providing airport transfers for the author…)

I wanted to find out.

The extensive, highly visible role of the Sue Neill-Fraser Support Group has never been properly reflected in the various media reports about the case. This multi-faceted group of women and men from around Tasmania are united in their firm belief that Neill-Fraser's conviction was an egregious miscarriage of justice.

Their most notable achievement - other than providing emotional and psychological support to Sue Neill-Fraser - has been keeping the case in the public spotlight with the basic proposition that the conviction failed the test of 'beyond reasonable doubt'.

Unmerciful in their criticism of Tasmania's criminal legal system, keen-eyed members of the Support Group have carefully deconstructed the case against her and found it wanting.

For example, then Support Group President Jennie Herrera wrote to then (since deceased) Attorney General Dr Vanessa Goodwin in October 2014 welcoming the announcement of plans to bring in the new Right to Further Appeal legislation, and included a number of concerning shortcomings in the trial. One concerned the CCTV footage from a Sandy Bay Road camera said to be 'leaving the scene of the crime' - "but the actual footage was not shown to the jury," wrote Herrara. "I was astonished when I saw the footage several years later and discovered that the driver was not visible, the number plate was not visible and it requires a leap of faith to determine that the vehicle was a Ford Falcon of which there are hundreds, probably thousands, in Hobart. And also that the footage was filmed at 12.25am."

Herrera then demonstrated why the timeline of events as proposed by the prosecution is a physical impossibility. Herrera and others in the Support Group have often shown acute detective skills.

They have protested her innocence in the streets of Hobart, in the precincts of Parliament and of the Court - but just as importantly, their very existence and perseverance has buoyed the spirits of the woman in Risdon Prison without a public voice of her own. Here, in the words of **Jennie Herrera** and **Lynn Giddings**, the Support Group's story is told.

OUR SUPPORT GROUP

When Sue Neill-Fraser first came up in the Hobart Magistrates Court several people came along to support Sue and her mother Helen, including Lynn Giddings, Rhoda Gill, and myself, Jennie Herrera. What we heard was an entirely circumstantial case, devoid of evidence. So we were very surprised to learn that it was to be sent to trial. Friends and supporters also came to the Criminal Court in 2010 to join Sue's family including her first husband Brett Meeker—and we all sat and listened to an equally circumstantial case. It was hard to accept some of the things we saw in that court room. The DPP showed a large knife to the jury and left it sitting in their full view for the rest of the trial but then he suggested a wrench, then a screw-driver, then a 'something' as a murder weapon. We, in our innocence, had always believed that assertions in a criminal trial have to be backed up by evidence.

"Should we be lobbying the government?"

When Sue was given a 26 year sentence it was hard to believe. Neither the Appeal nor the attempt to get the High Court to look at the case were successful—which members of the public often took as evidence of guilt without understanding that appeals look at mistakes in law, not the many problems there are with the adversarial trial process or with police investigations where police have focussed on 'the most likely person' rather than a thorough investigation of every aspect of a death.

But the difficulty for family, friends, and wider community concern was how to create support without making life in prison harder for Sue. Amanda Stark arranged a vigil at Marieville Esplanade on the anniversary of Bob Chappell's disappearance. Rebecca Harrison organised a get-together in the Botanical

Gardens to bring sympathetic people together. There was some confusion over just what a support group could or should do. Were we mainly there to visit and support Sue and her family? Should we be lobbying the government? Should we be raising money or just awareness? Should we be trying to find other information, in effect doing some sleuthing ourselves?

Only a few supporters had any legal knowledge and although many of us had been involved in activism or charity or community work we had never tried to overturn a conviction or get someone in Tasmania out of jail. As more people came forward to express their doubts about Sue's trial and conviction we could see that all these reasons for creating a support group were relevant. We began to hold regular meetings and to hold regular vigils. This made it easier for members of the public to come forward with offers of help.

Barbara Etter came forward to offer Sue pro bono legal help. Minneke Haynes donated the printing of thousands of leaflets which more than a dozen supporters letterboxed around the Greater Hobart area. Filmmaker Eve Ash produced her film 'Shadow of Doubt' which when shown in Hobart (and on Foxtel), and later sold on DVD, brought more people forward. A band in Melbourne called Grand Jury composed and produced a CD, and the idea of a play eventually resulted in a season in Hobart for the play called 'An Inconvenient Woman'. Three people in Melbourne put up $40,000 for a reward. Rosemary Phelps created a Facebook page and an email network for people who couldn't come to meetings. Lynn Giddings kept people in touch through regular news bulletins.

Although the government, police, and media showed little sympathy it became clear to us, through what people were offering and what they needed from us, that we needed a much more structured approach to supporting Sue and needed to be able to reassure people that donations would be fully accounted for and well-spent.

"information from public dismissed by police and DPP"

Rhoda Gill prepared a constitution and carried the process through Corporate Affairs for the support group to formally become an incorporated body, the Neill-Fraser Support Group, Inc. Over the years the group has had a number of presidents, secretaries, and treasurers, and has organised fund-raisers, particularly to pay for the hiring of billboards around Hobart, as well as rallies, vigils, film nights, and social events. We also purchased, or had donated, badges, t-shirts, and stickers.

We could dig out information that might throw new light on the case—for example,

a. the jury never learned that Richard King, who made the worrying phone call to Sue on the night Bob Chappell disappeared, and Philip Triffett who went to the police two days later to say Sue had tried to hire him as a 'hit man' knew each other and both lived on a country road north of Hobart, called Back Tea Tree Road.
b. that several people who had gone to the police or the DPP with information had been dismissed as irrelevant.
c. that a time-line of all that the Crown said Sue had done that night put in to the Crown's own time frame showed it simply wasn't possible.
d. that the yacht's EPIRB supposedly found by a man from Berriedale, Robert Macleary Page, on the 27th January 2009

and handed to Glenorchy Police had, according to Page, been found above the high water mark on Maning Avenue Beach.

e. that in less than 4 months, 3 middle-aged yachtsmen had gone into about a square mile of the Derwent and died; Peter Irwin found dead in the water at the Sandy Bay Yacht Club, a man found dead in the water at Constitution Dock, and Bob Chappell supposedly killed in the area between these two apparent drownings.

f. we learnt that what police said in court about homeless people not being at the shore that night were contradicted by their own log books

But we could see that there are two fundamental problems with the justice system in Australia:

1. Police, courts, and government departments, once a conviction is secured, have a vested interest in NOT looking at anything which might raise doubts. As the Council for Civil Liberties pointed out, even if Bob Chappell turned up alive it would not automatically get Sue out of prison. Supporters or families can pay private investigators but there is no realistic channel through which to pass any new information, and
2. although appeals can look at mistakes made by judges and lawyers there is no mechanism to look at the many problems which can lead to wrongful convictions. These include: poor forensic investigation, non-disclosure, mis-identification (eg. the 'female outline' supposedly seen by a John Hughes may well have been local yachtsman, Grant Maddocks, who had long hair in 2009), lying by police, lawyers, or witnesses, honest mistakes or confusions by witnesses as to times and places (eg. there was both a yacht and a catamaran called 'Four

> Winds' on the Derwent that day and both looked quite similar from side on—yet no witness was asked if they were sure they had seen the yacht rather than the catamaran), racism, sexism, the floating of rumours (including the still widespread rumour that Sue killed her first husband Brett Meeker) etc.

We arranged for Bob Moles, the Adelaide based legal academic and expert in miscarriages of justice, to visit Hobart and began lobbying the State Attorney-General, Dr Vanessa Goodwin, to bring in legislation that would allow for further appeals. We got nearly 2,000 signatures on a petition and about twenty supporters went to Parliament House to listen to the debates on the proposed bill. Eventually it was passed unanimously through both House of Parliament in 2015. Although we would have liked it to be stronger, it only allows for the very subjective 'new' and 'compelling' definition, it nevertheless meant that Sue could now apply for a new hearing once it was signed into law.

Barbara Etter was accused of 'Contempt of Court', solicitor Jeff Thompson was accused of 'Perverting the Course of Justice', two potential witnesses were also accused of 'Perverting the Course of Justice' which has meant that Sue's supporters have spent six months in and out of court in support of both Sue and those who have got caught up in the case. W.A. Barrister Tom Percy took on the case pro bono with the help of Melbourne lawyer Paul Galbally, a key reminder that high profile lawyers also have doubts about the safety of Sue's conviction.

'Sue turned my life around!'

Over the years supporters have come from two directions, those who believe absolutely in Sue's innocence and those who believe that there are sufficient problems with the police investigation and the court process for her conviction to be regarded as unsafe. In practice these two views tend to coalesce into dedicated support for Sue.

Unlike other kinds of campaigns the support group has brought together people from varying backgrounds. Sue herself was a member of the Young Liberals years ago, the parents of a former Labor premier give endless time and support, several passionate Greens members are committee members. Sue is an Anglican, her supporters include Catholics, Uniting Church people, Mormons, Quakers, and atheists. Although at times we have been unsure where best to put the group's time, effort and money, these problems have always been worked out amicably.

Although we occasionally get abused, the vast majority of people are sympathetic and interested. We hear a variety of possible scenarios from people who believe Bob Chappell is living the high life everywhere from the South of France to Bermuda to North Queensland, to the people who believe Bob's body was fed to pigs on a Derwent Valley farm to the man who thought he might have been stuffed in a fridge and dumped in the river. We hear from overseas visitors shocked to learn that a miscarriage of justice could occur in peaceful Tasmania. Sometimes girls who have been in prison with Sue rush up to us at vigils to give us a hug and say things like 'Sue turned my life around!'.

At the time of Sue's conviction the media implied she was a wealthy woman who got what she deserved. That has gradually changed. It is good to see media people, such as Charles Wooley, strongly in support of a new trial. And even people who were initially antagonistic, like Andrew Rule in Melbourne, have now taken a more sympathetic stance.

But the fact remains that our justice system has deep flaws and our greater awareness of these flaws is of little comfort. We continue to hope that we can both get Sue out of jail (*Sue was released on parole in October 2022*) and shine a light on aspects of Tasmanian justice which are careless, biased, incompetent, and even corrupt.

Historic overview compiled by Lynn Giddings

(Lynn is the mother of Lara Giddings, who wrote the Foreword)

On Friday night, 15 October 2010, when a Supreme Court jury found Susan Neill-Fraser 'guilty' of murdering Robert "Bob" Chappell, her partner of 18 years, her daughter, Sarah Bowles, told the press, "This is certainly not the last you'll see of us here, we're just going to keep fighting until we get Mum acquitted".

Sarah not only spoke for herself, her sister and her friends and family, she spoke for many of us who sat through the trial that had commenced on Tuesday, 21 September.

Sue's own words in her statement after Justice Alan Blow passed sentence, also resonated with many of us:

"I am disappointed in the way justice has been dispensed and I believe this case should concern every Australian person. If this can happen to me, it can happen to anyone."

Many of us were numb with disbelief. There was no body, no weapon, no motive, no eye witness, no confession and a trial that felt like one of speculation, innuendo and mockery.

But our attention was immediately drawn to the press reports the next day, 16 October, of the biggest cocaine haul in Queensland's history, about 800 km off the coast. A luxury catamaran, *Edelweiss* from South America had a *rendez-vous* with *Mayhem of Eden,* a sloop that had moored at Scarborough

Marina, the same marina where Sue and Bob had purchased their yacht, *Four Winds*. Pity the jury hadn't heard of this before considering their verdict; all they had heard was that Sue's 'drug theory' was rejected, quashing "speculation that drug smugglers could be responsible for the disappearance of a Hobart yachtsman" (*Mercury* 24 March 2009).

On 22/10/2010, Sue wrote a letter from,
Cell 2,

'The Primrose Path', Hell's Gates

Dear Everyone,
What wonderful support you have all given me; literally through 'thick and thin'. Don't really know how to thank you, except to say I am so very grateful. Most of us doubted that there could actually be a conviction, due to the small matter of a total lack of evidence. Now, with the new and notorious 'label' of 'convicted killer', ... I envisage a long struggle for justice, similar in some ways to the ordeal that Lindy Chamberlain was subjected to.

Without the love and support of Emma and Sarah, my wonderful daughters, their husbands, my mother and brother, extended family and a determined group of friends and supporters, I would not have had the strength to continue. As it is I will fight on with renewed determination, through all legal channels available to me.

I am so disappointed in the way justice has been dispensed in this matter and I believe it should concern every thinking person in Australia. If this can happen to me, it can happen to anyone, and although I understand that I must physically accept the court's judgement, I shall continue to protest my innocence most vehemently. I loved Bob deeply and would never have harmed him. I now place my faith in the appeal process and can only pray that in the fullness of time I will be vindicated.

Sue Neill-Fraser

I received a copy of Sue's two-page letter of which this represents a part. I do not know who else received it or how many copies were posted but Sue, herself, had picked us out as "a determined group of friends and supporters". This was our 'naming' moment.

In addition to the many court appearances in support and planned vigils, a group of the fitter supporters could pop up anywhere, alone or in pairs, mostly near traffic lights and mostly early in the morning to catch people going to work. Others letter-boxed suburbs around Hobart with Quaker pamphlets and postcards. Their tireless enthusiasm that is not recorded in the press needs mentioning.

However, I feel the final word should go to Jennie Herrera, the inspiration for the vigils. On Saturday, August 20, 2016, under the headline,

Persistent in push to acquittal for killer, the *Mercury* reporter Patrick Billings wrote:

> *Say what you will about supporters of convicted murderer Susan Neill-Fraser, there is no denying their persistence.*
>
> *A unanimous guilty verdict, failed appeal, High Court rejection, an unfavourable coroner's finding and a shaky new bid for freedom have done nothing to blunt their conviction that Neill-Fraser didn't kill her partner Bob Chappell.*

If anything, each setback serves to strengthen their belief that there's something wrong with the justice system and Neill-Fraser's 23-year jail sentence.

Holding a battered "Sue Neill-Fraser is innocent" sign, Jennie Herrera was yesterday among a handful of supporters in Hobart's CBD marking the seven years since her incarceration.

Ms Herrera is president of Neill-Fraser Support Group that has up to 30 members.

Ms Herrera said she would never give up on getting Neill-Fraser exonerated.

For Ms Herrera, who knew Neill-Fraser and her mother before the murder, it was the prosecution's time line. It never added up, she said.

Mr Chappell hasn't been seen since Australia Day 2009 when he disappeared from the couple's yacht moored in Sandy Bay.

"Strictly speaking, nobody knows that Bob Chappell is even dead," Ms Herrera said.

The group and their namesake are buoyed by the current case before the Supreme Court. It's being made possible under new right-to- appeal laws that allow for an acquittal or retrial if "fresh and compelling evidence" can be produced.

Since 2022, the President of the Sue Neill-Fraser Support Group has been Rosie Crumpton-Crook. Their website: savesue.com

In December 2022, the Sue Neill-Fraser Support Group stated that following her release on parole, it "remains committed to keeping Sue's case in the public eye and clearing her name. Group members are mindful that Sue is not the only person in Australia wrongfully convicted and consequently have said they will continue to explore avenues for broadening the group's agenda."

A DAY IN THE LIFE

My naïve request in the middle of 2021 to Sue Neill-Fraser (while awaiting the decision on her appeal) for a diary-like report on a typical day in prison provided readers of wrongfulconvictionsreport.org a fascinating insight into her life in prison – but resulted in her punishment. The letter passed through prison security without incident but she was placed in solitary confinement (that's the solitary confinement that Tasmanian prisons claim do not operate, according to prison officials). See if you can spot what she should not have revealed?

We wake each morning to the dulcet tones of a PA announcement, "This is your 6:45 wake up call" usually followed by the edifying news that we will be locked down for part or all of that day. Lockdowns are far more prevalent than they used to be, mostly due to lack of staff and during these phases, inmates can expect to be confined to their cells, buildings, or unit boundaries. I'm in a minimum rated area, so I have the good fortune to be able to get out in the fresh air and also have access to a computer most of the time.

We have gatherings, musters at different times each day to ensure no one has burrowed under or parachuted over the perimeter fence or heaven forbid, died in the night. Mind you, the fence is so high, one would need to build a trebuchet to sail over it.

Following the wake up call, I hop on an exercise machine for 20 minutes after which a posse of officers arrive to count us and our metal cutlery (in case it has been put to forbidden unspecified use), then showers and medication where the queue often stretches to Timbuktu. I take vitamins, so I also have to line up under the beady eye of a custodial officer who asks to look in your mouth to make sure the tablets have disappeared. Think fledglings in a nest begging for food.

There is a good reason for this. Some inmates are quite clever at concealing the tablets, then reminiscent of cormorants regurgitating and trafficking them to others. The first time I observed this process, I saw what appeared to be convulsive choking, and assuming it was the real thing, slapped the inmate's back, causing the tablets to fly forth across the room. The intended recipient pounced and thanking me explained what was going on.

Naturally, these antics swiftly led to increasingly bizarre behaviour, a dead giveaway, ensuring the issue is picked up quickly. We have another muster at nine euphemistically entitled, 'labor parade' where all inmates line up to be recounted in a common area. The real purpose of this is to make sure no one simply goes back to bed after medication to 'sleep their sentence away'.

Assuming no lockdown, inmates then disperse to their jobs, if they have one or attend courses. My official 'job title' is peer mentor, which entails assisting new inmates' inductions into the prison, explaining the rules and showing them the ropes. Unofficially, I help out with a range of issues. Tutoring, interpreting legal mail, correcting documents, writing inmates mitigation pleas, the list goes on. Having no legal training whatsoever, I was initially reluctant to become involved in this area.

However, I changed my mind after it became clear that some inmates were illiterate and unable to read, let alone interpret or reply to letters from their lawyers.

Others were not eligible for legal aid, a dire situation often affecting those already serving sentences, and then arraigned on fresh charges which didn't meet funding guidelines. Almost every morning, I'm approached usually in the medication line where there is no escape, with a request from someone who hasn't mastered the art of writing, or if they have, can't bring themselves to compose a document to anyone in authority without a liberal sprinkling of expletives. I'm handed a note along the lines of, *"if yer honour had effing well let me out the last two effing times, I wouldn't have belted the c***"* together with a muttered request, "*Can you fix it up Sue?*"

These diversions can take time to sort out. Recently, a sheaf of papers was thrust under my nose with an outrage, "*Yer gotta elp me. Me lawyer's no good, it just hung up on me.*" Well, no surprises there. Once I unearthed the facts for the prosecutor, it turned out the aggrieved, a well-known thief, had been charged with absconding from the supermarket with 42 tins of powdered sports drink concealed into her jacket and there was CCTV footage. "Did you take them?" "*Nah, I only steal meat and makeup.*" "Stop. I don't want to hear it." Having read hundreds of these missives destined for prosecutors, I'd long since reached the inescapable conclusion that significant flights of fancy could afflict the authors. In this case, I really didn't see how the small being in front of me could hide one tin, let alone 42 on her person. We wrote back, politely requesting a copy of the CCTV footage to verify this astonishing accusation. As predicted, the tape went missing and the charge dropped.

When arrested 12 years ago, I refused to believe such things occurred. Wiser now. As the morning wears away, there are frequent interruptions to relieve the monotony. People with a serious drug habit often come in looking skeletal, having omitted to eat much real food in the pursuit of 'ice', the most likely curse of their lives. Once clean, they then become ravenous, eating everything in sight. We in the minimum units are able to save some of our unused meals, cereals, et cetera, for cooking, a resource, which becomes very attractive to those who don't have access to it. With breakfast a distant memory, various hungry souls arrive from medium (*security*) to lurk at our front gate and reminiscent of a flock of predatory seagulls, screech appeals for leftovers. "*Ya got any biscuits? Meals? Eaten yer dessert yet? Do you want it or can I have it? What about an egg then?*" Anyone stepping outside with any sort of bowl or container immediately attracts the attention of a dozen pairs of eyes, which with shark like focus zoom in to determine whether something edible might be had.

At lunchtime, we are locked down for an hour, a time I use to rummage through legal precedents in the hope of finding useful information applicable to my case. I also make phone calls. I have two beautiful daughters and four grandchildren, and it really brightens my day if I can catch up with them. I find that I can no longer afford the self pitiful luxury of allowing myself to dwell on all that is lost. Long-held plans to introduce them to farm life, skiing, sailing, horse riding, all the good things we'd planned to do together. However, I can ask them about **their** day's activities; tadpole catching, model building, bike riding, maths homework (horrors!), and so on. Short, miserable, cold days and grey skies, dismal features of Tasmanian winters are once again upon us. So much of my time is currently spent out of the icy chill undercover.

Ridiculous as it sounds, I never seem to have any spare hours in the day. By the time I finish one document and begin the next, it's time for the five o'clock evening lockdown. In summer, any spare time was spent in the vegetable garden, weeding, planting, watering, pruning. It's restful for the soul away from the noise and drama that is part and parcel of prison life. Years ago, I began a seed saving program, a resource which continues to provide a good supply of greens, which we then harvest then cook to compliment the dreaded 'chill meals' supplied by the prison. We no longer get any fresh fish, only the Besser block grey, heavily battered variety of, I suspect, dubious provenance (scurrilous offerings from Northern neighbours). So, I take fish oil instead, much safer and dream of sushi.

One of the saddest things I see in prison is the incarceration of people due to mental health issues. It occurs with monotonous regularity and although the custodial officers of the prison are supportive and do their best to engage, timely professional intervention remains far from our shores. Our time is pretty much circumscribed and there isn't a great deal of intellectual stimulation.

Due to COVID, visits have been kept one a week instead of the usual three and I really miss the interaction at times feeling as if I'm caught up in a kind of existential Groundhog Day existence. Connection to the outside world is vital to combating this malaise. However, it's tempered by the realisation that visiting the Risdon Riviera, as I call it, is not everyone's cup of tea. In fact, for some it's nervous breakdown territory. Just navigating security can be an ordeal. Sniffed by dogs, lined up in queues with other visitors, some of whose only use for a bar of soap has been to grease lock mechanisms to ease the way of picking them. All a bit grim, and I will remain very grateful to all those who continued to make the effort, some for over a decade. So, for now, life plods on; more 'stolen' years ticking away.

ANNEXURE A – INTEGRITY COMMISSION TASMANIA

Object and objectives, Integrity Commission Act 2009

1. The object of this Act is to promote and enhance standards of ethical conduct by public officers by the establishment of an Integrity Commission.
2. The objectives of the Integrity Commission are to –
   a. improve the standard of conduct, propriety and ethics in public authorities in Tasmania; and
   b. enhance public confidence that misconduct by public officers will be appropriately investigated and dealt with; and
   c. enhance the quality of, and commitment to, ethical conduct by adopting a strong, educative, preventative and advisory role.
3. The Integrity Commission will endeavour to achieve these objectives by –
   a. educating public officers and the public about integrity; and
   b. assisting public authorities deal with misconduct; and
   c. dealing with allegations of serious misconduct or misconduct by designated public officers; and
   d. making findings and recommendations in relation to its investigations and inquiries.

Integrity Commission Tasmania has rebuffed all complaints relating to the case of Sue Neill-Fraser.

Inadmissible forensic evidence complaint

The High Court's dismissal of Sue Neill-Fraser's application seeking leave to appeal (August 12, 2022) leaves unresolved the matter of inadmissible forensic evidence at trial and the lack of disclosure of that error to the courts. Flinders University legal academic Dr Bob Moles took the matter to the Integrity Commission Tasmanian (ICT), pointing out the legal obligation that remains unfulfilled.

Moles says the correspondence rejecting his submission reveals that the ICT appears not to understand that "the use of evidence which is false and misleading undermine the rule of law and represent a fundamental breach of our international human rights obligations."

Dr Bob Moles to Integrity Commission August 1, 2022 (extracts)

Of course, the FSST is not concerned about the outcome of the appeal. It should only be concerned to inform the DPP's office that in this case evidence was given at trial by the forensic scientist which was not in accordance with appropriate scientific standards and was therefore inadmissible.

It will then be for the DPP's office to determine what to make of that from a legal perspective. It clearly has not been appropriate for FSST, having been made aware of these problems for some years now, to remain inactive or unconcerned about the consequences which have arisen from their failure to provide proper scrutiny of evidence being provided by their employees.

As the Splatt and Morin reports make clear, where error has occurred all those involved have an ethical obligation to ensure that it is corrected. That obligation is continuing until the error is corrected.

I note that the Integrity Commission of Tasmania has the power to recommend to the Premier the establishment of a Commission of Inquiry under the Commissions of Inquiry Act 1995. There clearly should be an inquiry into the provision of forensic services in Tasmania, as the errors in this case are indicative of systemic failures which might well affect other cases.

Summary of issues arising:

1. Why did the Director of FSST not respond to the report which was sent to him raising concerns about the forensic evidence in the case of Susan Neill-Fraser?
2. Why did the Director of FSST not conduct an inquiry into the issues which were raised in the report which was submitted to him?
3. Why did the Director of FSST refer the report to the Asst Commission in TasPOL when the issues raised were of a forensic and scientific nature?
4. Was the reference of the report to TasPOL a breach of the policy of FSST to maintain an operational separation between FSST and TasPOL?
5. Why did FSST not conduct proper peer review of the reports issued by the forensic scientist and of the evidence which was given in an important murder trial?

6. The evidence of the forensic scientist in relation to DNA and that of the pathologist in relation to death being caused by a blow to the head should not have been admitted at trial. It did not comply with the conditions for admissibility of expert evidence. Although the provision of this evidence was no fault of those providing it (they were subject to directions by the judge or prosecutor), they do have an obligation to inform the prosecution (post trial) that the evidence should not have been admitted and may have been misleading to the jury.

Duty of disclosure: The relevant legal principles require the Crown (which includes the prosecutors, police and any other agencies of the state (expert witnesses) in support of a prosecution, to disclose any materials which are relevant to the case presented by the prosecution. It is particularly important that any material or information which might undermine the prosecution case or the integrity of an expert witness be disclosed.

The duty of disclosure is continuing – it continues after the trial and after all appeals have been concluded.

Integrity Commission reply to Dr Bob Moles August 12, 2002 (extract)

We have carefully considered whether the allegations could amount to misconduct, as defined in section 4 of the Integrity Commission Act (the Act). This is important, as we can only act in relation to a complaint that alleges misconduct. We are also required to focus on possible misconduct that is serious or involves senior public officers.

It is clear from your complaint and your academic work that you are concerned with various aspects of the evidence used in the trial of Ms Neill-Fraser.

However, the information that you have provided is an academic opinion and does not indicate that misconduct is likely to have occurred. I note your views and commentary on the need for the independence of FSST. However I do not consider this to be an issue relating to possible misconduct, as defined in the Act.

In the circumstances, I have decided that due to the low likely culpability of the public officers involved it is not in the public interest for us to investigate the complaint. I have decided to dismiss your complaint, under section 36(1)(f) of the Act.

Thank you for bringing this matter to our attention.

Michael Easton
Chief Executive Officer
Integrity Commission Tasmania

Dr Bob Moles responds to Integrity Commission August 22, 2022 (complete):

Thank you for your letter of 12 August. I regret to say that the opinions which it expresses appear to be lacking in both common-sense and logic.

Academic opinion

You indicate that I am putting to you a mere 'academic opinion' which you obviously rate lower on the scale of human endeavour than the opinions of others, without explaining why that is so. I need hardly point out that the research output of universities is more highly regarded outside of Tasmania.

Indeed, my opinion was sought as 'expert advice' to the Goudge Judicial Inquiry in Canada, as it was on the establishment of a Criminal Review Commission also in Canada. In addition, our latest book on criminal appeals (to which I referred in my submission to you) was commissioned by the internationally respected law publisher LexisNexis and was published by their legal practitioner's division as a reference work for legal practitioners.

However, the more important point is that the content of my letter to you was not to provide you with my opinions, but with reference to the judgments of the courts in Australia, Britain and Canada. The empirical basis for my submission to you was the transcript of the trial of Ms Neill-Fraser. Everything I said about the trial was supported by references to that transcript, and so it can hardly be said to contain, in that respect, any expression of my opinions.

The judgments which relate to the evaluation of the propositions put forward in that transcript are not mine, but those based upon the judgments of the courts of the United Kingdom in the IRA bombing cases – the judgment of a judge of the Supreme Court of Canada - and within my report, the judgment of the Supreme Court of Victoria. Of course, all of that is backed up by the sections of our book on the admissibility of expert opinions and the conduct of prosecutors in Australian courts, to which I also referred in my submission to you and which, for convenience, I repeat below. Nobody has ever suggested that we have misrepresented the law on any of those issues in any way.

No indication of 'misconduct'

I was then surprised to learn that you formed the view that the matters which I raised with you do not even raise a prima facie case of 'misconduct having occurred' so as to warrant any inquiry by the Integrity Commission. It is clear that the judgments of the Australian courts to which I referred took a very different view. They make it clear that the securing of wrongful convictions by the use of evidence which is false and misleading undermine the rule of law and represent a fundamental breach of our international human rights obligations.

I had provided you with the references to the Australian legal judgments which used the expressions 'an extremely grave criminal offence' and 'criminality at the extreme end of the spectrum of official corruption'. The Lord Chief Justice of England and Wales on a visit to Sydney described the possibility of a person being wrongly convicted of a serious crime as constituting a 'catastrophic failure' of the legal system.

Yet you state that the conduct to which I have referred is 'not serious' - in the context of the possibility of a woman having been wrongly imprisoned for over 13 years. This is your response to the allegation that Forensic Science Services in Tasmania failed to provide peer review of the false and misleading evidence before being provided to the court; failed to investigate that misconduct when it was brought to their attention in my report; failed to maintain operational independence from the police in respect of investigating the concerns which I had raised; failed in their duty to the court to investigate if disclosable material (false evidence) was required to be disclosed to the DPP or the courts.

My conclusion

I have to say that I respectfully disagree with your assessment. The circumstances to which I have referred, when they occurred in the UK, led to two major Commissions of Inquiry, and the most important structural reform to law enforcement which has ever occurred in that jurisdiction – the introduction of a Criminal Cases Review Commission.

Yet when similar misconduct is reported to you, some 30 years after the UK catastrophe was exposed, the Integrity Commission of Tasmania is not embarrassed by publicly stating that they see no need to investigate even the possibility of a similar catastrophe having occurred in your jurisdiction.

I have no doubt that the opinions which you have expressed in your letter to me will be found wanting, either at the subsequent inquiry into the operations of the Integrity Commission, or the inquiry which I have no doubt will also occur into the shocking misconduct which has occurred in the case of Ms Neill-Fraser.

In the meantime, I would suggest that it would do no harm for the Integrity Commission to reconsider its position in relation to this issue while it still has the chance to do so.

***(signed)* Dr Robert Moles ACII (UK) LLB (Hons) (Belf) PhD (Edin)**

Misleading Statement by Assistant Police Commissioner complaint

In August 2019, Integrity Commission Tasmania also dismissed the complaint by the author against *Assistant Police Commissioner Richard Cowling. That complaint raised the* contradiction between his statement to the media and the summary of facts presented in court, regarding Meaghan Vass recanting her statement made on *60 Minutes* (March 10) in which she admitted witnessing a fight involving Bob Chappell and stating Sue Neill-Fraser was not there.

"The legislation which establishes the Commission only allows us to investigate 'misconduct' – which has a specific definition under the Integrity Commission Act (2009) (the Act)," replied Integrity Commission Director Operations, Michael Easton.

"While it is clear from your complaint, that you are concerned about the actions of Tasmania Police, the information you have provided does not indicate that misconduct, as defined in the Act, has occurred."

1. If the definition of 'misconduct' in the Act excludes reference to police making misleading and prejudicial statements the definition probably needs to be improved.
2. My complaint was lodged in the absence of any evidence to support Assistant Commissioner Richard Cowling's statement. Such a statement at such a time in the protracted case of Sue Neill-Fraser could be expected to be supported by at least an excerpt from the relevant interview with Meaghan Vass, to which he refers.
3. Assistant Commissioner Richard Cowling's public statement was issued prior to the March 21 hearing before Justice Brett in the Neill-Fraser appeal process. If his statement was factual and the DPP was not briefed to advise the court, Justice Brett would no doubt regard that failure very seriously. Is it not perverting justice? Is it likely contempt of court?
4. After Commander Cowling's statement, I sought a response from Meaghan Vass: no, she did not recant her *60 Minutes* version when interviewed by police.

COMPLAINTS BY EVE ASH & COLIN MCLAREN

Literally dozens of allegations have been lodged with Integrity Commission Tasmania over the years by documentarian Eve Ash and former homicide taskforce leader and author Colin McLaren related to the Sue Neill-Fraser case. No decisions were made for almost four years because Sue's case was before the court. Then after Sue lost her appeal in November 2021 when able to decide, the ITC said too much time had elapsed. The complaints were resubmitted and updated with ten new allegations presented in 2022.

All the complaints have been dismissed by ICT with a statement that said, in part:

> *... our assessment has shown that there is no substance to the allegations of misconduct, as defined in the Act, and that many of the allegations have already been raised and tested in Court and/or by the Coroner. Of the remaining allegations, they relate to less serious misconduct that allegedly occurred over 10 years ago. Two of the officers are now retired. An investigation of the conduct of the officers involved would be an unjustifiable use of public resources.*

Ash is not satisfied. "The court and the Coroner that rubber stamped the court outcome were not a test of our complaints.

Second, how dare they talk about retired officers and unjustifiable use of public resources when a woman has spent 13 years in jail for no good reason in their state under their watch. And three, at least our complaints are well documented when a FULL Inquiry or Royal Commission finally shows what a shameful travesty this whole thing is."

A few samples of the complaints, as compiled by Eve Ash in her 29 part podcast, Who Killed Bob?;

- We said there was an inept police investigation, ignoring several persons of interest. Police failed to interview key witnesses. Two criminals with long police records were in the vicinity at the time, not interviewed until 2 years after Sue was convicted.
- We complained that one of those criminals, in a yacht next to the Four Winds, was helped by a DPP representative the day before appearing in court for Sue's leave to appeal, to establish the position of his yacht as one km away when it was only 100-200m away from the Four Winds on Australia Day night.
- We advised that a detective who collected evidence, the red jacket, then LOST it and 3 days later found it lying around the police parking garage. In court he said he handed the jacket in for forensic testing with no mention that he broke the chain of custody and sent a contaminated jacket for testing.
- We listed non-disclosure of records in relation to Meaghan Vass, whose DNA was at the crime scene.
- And a policewoman, who used to be Meaghan's babysitter, did not report her involvement in a burglary around the time of the murder.

- And we said that after the DNA match, Det Sinnitt never interviewed Meaghan Vass about her whereabouts on the night of Bob's disappearance, even after discovering she had lied and had no alibi for the night of the murder. He never interviewed Meaghan's associates – and nothing was disclosed about the young male offenders who broken into boats, that Inspector Powell told me about when I interviewed him.
- We said a lot about TasPol losing evidence, not testing items, flawed forensic procedures, forensic reports with gaping holes of key evidence like the missing blue face-washer that was right next to the Vass DNA. It was lost. Never tested. And two other vomit rages never tested.
- And this one is such tunnel vision. A so-called weather-beaten man was seen by Jane Austin in an inflatable dinghy near the Four Winds the evening of Bob Chappell's disappearance – she said he had stocky build, late 40s, early 50s, short reddish brown wavy hair, not close shaven. He was never investigated, because police decided that the description of the man matched Sue Neill-Fraser.
- We said that TasPol improperly seized exhibits from Jeff Thompson, the lawyer, and misused their authority tapping phones, accessing privileged defence information, improperly seizing documentary evidence and improperly charging individuals with perverting the course of justice.
- We said that Taspol were targeting Colin McLaren and myself by falsely alleging we took part in perverting the course of justice in the lead-up to Sue's leave to Appeal application.

Integrity Commission Tasmania's questionable decisions in all matters related to the case of Sue Neill-Fraser, appear to be in keeping with the objectives evident in the Attorney-General's office, the Legal Profession Board and the TasPol hierarchy: protect the conviction.

ANNEXURE B - THE ILLOGICAL CONVICTION

As if all the legal arguments weren't enough, the prosecution's case is damned at the start by the absence of logic, as explained in this 3-part analysis by Benjamin Dean BSc. Benjamin Dean observed the trial at the Supreme Court of Tasmania in October 2010 and has followed the case ever since. He has a BSc, having studied the natural sciences and computing. He has a strong philosophical interest in cultural epistemology, and its evolutionary advantage.

PART 1

What remains compelling about the conviction of Sue Neill-Fraser is that the guilty verdict contradicts the rules for a valid inference in formal logic. And since a contradiction renders the conclusion false, the State of Tasmania neither recognised the essential premises necessary to validly infer guilt in this trial, nor presented the necessary evidence for establishing these essential facts. And by convicting Sue Neill-Fraser, the State of Tasmania, has effectively abandoned the democratic obligations to the principles of equality in law, in a nation that is a signatory to UN Convention on Human Rights.

no proof of death

In August 2009, when the Tasmania Police, with the endorsement of the Director of Public Prosecutions, charged and remanded Sue Neill-Fraser for murdering her partner Bob Chappell, the State of Tasmania held insufficient evidence, as revealed at the October 2010 trial, to establish whether Bob Chappell was dead, let alone prove with evidence his manner of death as murder. That is, there was an absence of evidentiary proof for establishing the Major Premise of the crime - an essential fact for a valid inference of guilt.

In contrast to the trial transcript in which the words murder/s/er/ing/ed and kill/er/ing appear some 350 times, the Crown presented to the jury, no body, no eyewitnesses to a murder, no confession, no murder weapon, no established motive, and no forensic evidence that could rationally eliminate all competing hypotheses for establishing why Bob Chappell had disappeared from the *Four Winds* yacht, on Australia Day 2009. As expressed by legal academic, Dr Robert Moles of Flinders University, there was "…no compelling evidence to show that Bob Chappell is dead, let alone murdered"[1].

In explaining this absence of evidence for establishing the Major Premise of the charge to which Sue Neill-Fraser was Commanded by Authority to answer, the former Crown Prosecutor, Tim Ellis SC, in the July 27, 2015, edition of the *Australian Women's Weekly*, suggested; *"It was not and is not essential to the valid conviction of Ms Neill-Fraser that the prosecution produce a murder weapon or prove a manner of death".*

However, the Crown Prosecution's appeal for validity to support this conviction, contradicts formal logic, namely the rule for a valid inference modus ponens (if p, then q). Whereby, one fact as the Major Premise (p) MUST be proven with sufficient evidence as true, before it is rational to infer another fact to know if ANY perpetrator (q) exists, as a rational conclusion. That is, to know whether or not, ANY Perpetrator/s (q) exists, the truth value of this fact is logically conditional on whether the premise of the crime (p), has been established with sufficient evidence (or not).

In the absence of evidence to know if Bob Chappell is dead, let alone murdered, then ALL people are innocent is the valid conclusion in formal logic.

The result being that the charge and remand of Sue Neill-Fraser in August 2009 was arbitrary because it lacked a valid reason, by contradicting the rule modus ponens, and therefore was not rationally possible for the Tasmania Police, or the DPP to logically know the existence of ANY perpetrator to the crime of murder. The action violated Article 9 of the International Covenant on Civil and Political Rights. The Burden of Proof, could not logically be met by modus ponens, and therefore no valid reason existed for arresting Sue Neill-Fraser (or ANYONE) for the murder of Bob Chappell in August 2009.

The Tasmania Police investigation was deficient and lacked sufficient evidence necessary to establish the major Premise for the Crime, albeit Tasmania's justice system remains satisfied with a 23 year sentence for Sue Neill-Fraser, to a crime yet to be established in evidence.

Consequently, what is compelling (in a bad way), is that the conviction of Sue Neill-Fraser has effectively normalised a legal process in the State of Tasmania, in which the premises necessary to validly infer guilt, are now being considered not necessary to be established in evidence in criminal cases, by either the Tasmania Police nor the Tasmanian Courts.

How are people equal before the court, if the standard of proving guilt *Beyond a Reasonable Doubt*, is accepted by the Court, but at the same time inherently doubtful due to the contradiction to the most basic of rules for a valid inference in formal logic.

How is the standard for the presumption of innocence being upheld by the State of Tasmania, if a crime is not required to be established with evidence? It is rationally not a fair court, if anyone can be sentenced to imprisonment, for a specific crime, yet to be established in evidence? Reason, it appears, is not available as a defence to those defending a criminal charge in Tasmania's Courts.

logic as necessary standard

This case dictates an urgent need for overhauling Tasmania's legal system. When Nicholas Cowdery KC, the former NSW director of public prosecutions, gave reasons not to prosecute Chris Dawson for the murder of Lyn Dawson[2], and those reasons logically contradict the Tasmania DPP decision to prosecute Sue Neill-Faser, then Australian Law is in need of adopting an explicit model of logic as a necessary standard to justify decisions as rational, and not based simply on belief. While the Tasmanian Government continues to waste this crisis by expressing full confidence in the State Legal System, they are complicit in the continued violation of fundamental Human Rights, allowing the propagating of these errors in other Tasmanian criminal trials, which is effectively undermining Australia as a legitimate democracy.

1. Dr Robert N Moles ACII (UK) LLB (Hons) (Belf) PhD (Edin), Adjunct Principal Researcher, College of

Humanities, Arts and Social Sciences, Flinders University, South Australia. – review of Shadow of Doubt, 16 July 2013 - Bob Moles' review *Shadow of Doubt* [Sue Neill-Fraser case, Tasmania] " ... no compelling evidence to show that Bob Chappell is dead, let alone murdered. " p1. Accessed 24/08/20.

2. Nicholas Cowdery KC, former NSW director of public prosecutions, giving reasons to not prosecute Chris Dawson for the murder of Lyn Dawson. "Without a body, without knowing first of all whether in fact she is dead, without knowing secondly if she is dead, how she died, it's very hard to mount a case of a reasonable prospect of conviction just on motive and the undefined existence of means and opportunity. That makes it very weak," https://mobile.abc.net.au/news/2018-09-10/australian-story-who-killed-lyn-dawson/10213690?pfmredir=sm&nw=0 accessed 24/08/20

PART 2

To validly infer guilt, at least in the circumstantial case of Bob Chappell's disappearance, it is to argue logical converse equivalence between the crime and a perpetrator. This can be formally expressed by the Propositional Logic conditional (p ⊠ q). Which equates to ((if p, then q) AND (if q, the p)), meaning all p's are q's and all q's are p's only. In other words, all the circumstances of this Crime (p) point to this Perpetrator (q) <u>only</u>. Consistent with the evidence, no reasonable alternative can exist, without falsifying the conclusion of guilt, is validated by this conditional inference. The validity (of the argument structure) is dependent on the logical converse equivalence in truth values between the rules, ((if p, then q) AND (if q, then p only)).

Functionally, it is to establish in evidence three essential premises. Firstly, the Major Premise for the crime, necessary for knowing type, place and time. Secondly, the connection of a perpetrator to a crime in time and space, and thirdly, all the facts are consistent with the perpetrator acting alone. Similarly, an uncoerced and detailed confession could be of the quality to show logical equivalence between the crime (p) and a perpetrator (q), and in effect establishing the three essential premises.

accused was not at the crime scene

Yet despite some 700 hours of audio surveillance by Tasmania Police of Sue Neill-Fraser, her family, and visiting friends, no confession and none of these Essential Premises necessary for the conviction to make any sense, were established in evidence. There was no proof for the 'manner of death', necessary for establishing the type of crime as murder, or to know for certain the place of the crime was on the *Four Winds* yacht, or to infer when. There was no compelling evidence to place Neill-Fraser on the yacht, and all evidence of others on the yacht, has to date been effectively disregarded as irrelevant by the Court.

Ignoring the hurdle of inferring the *Four Winds* as the place of the crime, because then there was an absence of evidence to know if Bob Chappell was dead, let alone murdered. There was insufficient evidence to place Neill-Fraser on the yacht. At trial in 2010, the defence argued to the trial Judge, that there was no case to answer, because of this paucity of evidence to establish the essential facts[1].

If the accused was not at the crime scene that is compelling evidence of innocence. And to distinguish between the innocent and the guilty, it is a necessary burden on a fair court to provide evidence to prove who in fact was present on the yacht. Otherwise, in the absence of evidence placing Neill-Fraser on the *Four Winds* yacht, there is no case to answer.

The trial judge effectively dismissed the argument. And thanks to the nature of legal precedent, the judge has thus effectively normalised a process in which even if an accused is not proved to be at a crime scene, that is not considered a valid reason to be presumed innocent in the State of Tasmania.

Furthermore, while there is any outstanding evidence of others on the *Four Winds* yacht, then the conclusion of guilt is false, in accordance with Propositional logic Bi-conditional rules for a valid inference, since all the circumstances cannot rationally point only to the accused. The significance of this evidence has become a tournament between State Authority and the People of Tasmania, when in fact, it indicates the deficiency with the original investigation.

In the absence of sufficient evidence to establish the Essential Premises, the Crown used a common fallacy for arguing guilt, recognised formally as Affirming the Consequent, or Converse Error. In which the prosecution implied guilt, by conversely showing Neill-Fraser as the perpetrator (q), because of her lies, red herrings, confused alibi, broken relationship, knowledge of boats, a cut hand, red jacket etc. [2], implying murder (p) was Bob Chappell's manner of death. It is fallacious because one can be a perpetrator to many acts, and murder not necessary any of those acts. To be a valid inference, it must be shown to have converse logical equivalence, in which the formal expression ((if p then q) and (if q then p)) becomes the Test on Evidence to determine logical equivalence.

For example, to Test evidence of a lie to validly infer a murderer, as was suggested by the Crown Prosecution's multiple lie references at trial, then converse logical equivalence (in truth values) must exist between the two propositions; All murderers (p) are liars (q), AND all liars (q) are murderers (p) only. If, and only if, both propositions are true, then evidence of a lie is a valid inference for identifying a murderer, and a conviction would be the correct conclusion.

If on the other hand, on average all people lie, and in the great majority of times for reasons other than having murdered someone, then the inference is fallacious, and the implication of a lie indicating a murderer is prejudicial of the truth. 'All liars are only murderers', is far from the truth, and the inference has no logical converse equivalence.

Similarly, the presentation of the presumptive results of glowing luminol to infer blood in the yacht's tender, in the absence of a confirmatory test for blood is prejudicial of the truth simply because many common substances will make luminol glow. The necessity of a confirmatory test is to validate logical converse equivalence (in truth values, (p ⊠ q)) between both the glow of luminol and the presence of blood.

Inspector Peter Powell identified seven pieces of evidence as key to the case in a TasPol media release[3]. An injury to her hand, being one he believed to be compelling evidence for guilt. Inferring if anyone was to murder someone then some type of injury is inevitable. This inference is fallacious because the great majority of injuries to all people are for reason other than having murdered someone. Evidence of an injury, has no logical converse equivalence to infer murder only. It is simply the Affirmation of the Consequent of Neill-Fraser being a perpetrator, and fails to establish murder as the necessary condition to have a perpetrator. Most of the key evidence identified by the Chief Investigator

Inspector Peter Powell fallaciously Affirmed the Consequent (fails to prove the crime).

The Tasmanian Court continues to uphold this fallacious argument to determine guilt. A court that determines guilt by a fallacious argument, where the truth has been lost, cannot rationally be considered a fair court. The imprisonment of Sue Neill-Fraser was a continuing violation of fundamental Human Rights by the State of Tasmania.

1. Tasmania v Neill-Fraser (2010) TASSC Evidence repeated references throughout the trial.
2. Tasmania v Neill-Fraser (2010) TASSC p1064 - 1081
3. https://www.police.tas.gov.au/news-events/media-releases/tasmania-police-statement-2-susan-neill-fraser-case/

PART 3

Justice Brett in granting Sue Neill-Fraser the right to appeal her 2010 conviction suggested the original case against the applicant was entirely circumstantial, and could properly be described as "strands in the cable".

Similarly, the Court of Criminal Appeal at her first appeal in 2012, described the case as the '…accumulation of the evidence, …none of which alone would justify a finding of guilt', but in '… combination was highly probative of guilt'[2].

If the 'strands in a cable' can properly describe the reasoning behind this entirely circumstantial case, then exactly how is the cogency of this analogy more precise for determining the truth, when there is an absence of evidence to prove "a manner of death"[3] as the Major Premise of the crime, which formally contradicts a valid inference of guilt, and therefore implies the violation of fundamental Human Rights, as was argued in part 1.

If an analogy can properly describe a form of reasoning for a conclusion of guilt to be the correct answer, then the assumptions of the analogy must be in agreement with formal systems of reasoning. The assumption of the evidence being that 'strands in a cable', accumulate to strengthen the cable, implying that confidence in the conclusion is increased by this accumulation.

pseudo science

However, if evidence, '...none of which alone would justify a finding of guilt', because singularly it can only indicate some degree of plausibility for a hypothesis of guilt, then the analogy assumes, by combination, an exclusivity for strengthening the conclusion of guilt. But this exclusivity of functionality is contradicted by the mathematics of probability. The combination of probabilities is not only complex, highly unintuitive, but it does not exclusively increase the likelihood of a hypothesis being correct when multiple probabilities are combined. It can be quite the opposite whereby the combination of probabilities can rapidly decay towards zero chance of the hypothesis being correct.

The analogy contradicts mathematics because with the combination of evidence, each piece indicating some plausible or probability of guilt is also the accumulation of every alternative explanation, equating to the degree of likelihood that <u>innocence</u> is the correct conclusion. To disregard the accumulation of alternative hypotheses (innocence), which the assumption of the 'strands in a cable' implicitly denies, is what Karl Popper described as **pseudo science. It is a method of accumulating**

evidence that confirms a hypothesis, while erroneously disregarding any evidence that contradicts the hypothesis.

Furthermore, within probability mathematics, if events are linked, in so far as one event must occur before another event can occur, and evidence cannot prove beyond a probability that each event did in fact occur, then the likelihood of guilt being a correct hypothesis mathematically becomes a fraction of a fraction in a chance of being the correct conclusion. This linking of probabilities was the case with the absence of evidence to place Neill-Fraser on the *Four Winds* yacht.

In 2012, when the Court of Criminal Appeal (CCA) accepted the Prosecution's hypothesis that Neill-Fraser through violence, killed Bob Chappell on the Four Winds yacht, winched his body into a dinghy and, having weighed it down, then disposed of it in the Derwent River4, they accepted an explanation that was absent of evidence to establish if Sue Neill-Fraser was on the yacht, and absent of evidence to establish 'a manner of death'. That is, the Prosecution's hypothesis, mathematically, had a fraction of a fraction of a chance to be correct, due to this absence of evidence.

The CCA, although mandated with determining if a miscarriage of justice had occurred, failed to interrogate these essential facts to ensure them established as unbroken links, necessary to rationally justify any explanation of the events.

cognitive bias

Similarly, both the Court and the police failed to recognise the importance of prior probability in assessing evidence. For instance, at trial the multiple references of Sue Neill-Fraser's broken relationship with Bob Chappell. The Crown Prosecution wanting to establish this as fact was '…relevant because it makes it more likely that she committed murder.'[5] However, the relevance of this fact is conditional on prior probabilities. If Australia has a murder rate of 2 per 100,000 per annum, and in the absence of evidence to '…prove a manner of death', then the prior probability is in the great majority of all people who break up in any given year, murder will not be the outcome. This 'relevance' from this evidence is predictive of the cause only to the murderers of the 2 people, and not to the rest of the +99.9% of individuals who break up without murdering their partners. Yet this 'relevant' evidence was presented from the beginning to the end of the trial. Much of the evidence presented at trial ignored prior probability. So the question is, what is regarded as unfair prejudice in a Court of Law if this type of evidence is considered probative.

This neglect of base rate or prior probability is regarded as a cognitive bias, which was championed by the Nobel prize winning psychologist and economist Daniel Kahneman, yet nonetheless embraced by an institution entrusted with determining the liberty of people within our Democracy.

The conviction of Sue Neill-Fraser questions the Tasmanian Court's methodology for determining what is true. If all people are equal before the court, then judgements of guilt cannot be based on a probability of guilt. That is, the Principles of Equality in Law cannot be upheld, if guilt is determined as a *likely* explanation of the circumstances. It makes no logical sense to prove guilt to be beyond a reasonable doubt, by a method that quantifies the size of doubt, but not the elimination of doubt, since any error equates to every chance for a miscarriage of justice to occur. All the circumstantial evidence cannot point only to the accused if it is not the only possible explanation of the circumstances. If judgements of guilt are being determined as the *most likely* conclusion, then all decisions by the Court, will have an inherent chance for a miscarriage of justice to occur.

judicial self-review

Australian law needs to recognise that the determination of guilt must be based on a deductive analysis, in which the essential premises are identified, and the necessary evidence is obtained by sufficient investigation to establish these essential facts. The conclusion of guilt must be the only rational explanation of the circumstances. For this reason, criminal trials in Australia should explicitly adhere to the rules for a valid inference in formal logic.

Judicial self review, and the limitations created by referencing itself to solve dilemmas in judgements, has meant the process of law has failed to embrace the exponential expansion of knowledge in intelligent analysis developed and used in other disciplines. The irony is, the failure of a Judicial Process translates as the tragedy of incarcerating the innocent, which seems to be considered less important than admitting error, or the concern voiced for the failure of precision in functionality within more benign products of our society. In a properly functioning Democracy, Justice should be on the cutting edge for recognising the tools for intelligent analysis, the rules for a valid argument, and recognising cognitive biases. Instead it is an institution tethered to the past, and rapidly losing respect for upholding the Principles of a Democracy, by an absence of leadership to design and the flexibility to learn from errors that lead to miscarriages of justice within our Court system. This case dictates the necessity for an overhaul of Tasmanian Justice, without which the State of Tasmania continues to violate fundamental Human Rights, within our Democracy, a signatory to UN Charters.

1. Neill-Fraser v Tasmania(2019) TASSC 10
2. Neill-Fraser v Tasmania [2012] TASCCA 2.
3. July 27th 2015 edition of the Australian Womens Weekly that; *"It was not and is not essential to the valid conviction of Ms Neill-Fraser that the prosecution produce a murder weapon or prove a manner of death".*
4. Neill-Fraser v Tasmania [2012] TASCCA 2
5. Tasmania v Neill-Fraser (2010) TASSC p153

Formal Logic can be described as the science for a valid inference, and Aristotle is generally considered the Founding Father. Formal logic has traditionally focused on deductive (either true or false) reasoning. Validity is related to the structure or form of an argument, and not concerned about the content/premises of the argument form. In an argument, if the content (or premises) are true statements, and the form is valid, then the argument is considered sound, and the conclusion can be guaranteed true. Without this mathematical precision in formal logic, modern computing could not exist.

EPILOGUE

There's plenty of blame to go round. Ground Zero, as it were, was the courtroom where the trial took place. Readers may agree with me that neither the prosecution, nor the defence nor indeed the judge served the interests of justice.

Chappell's body has never been found. The murder weapon – supposedly a heavy wrench – was a speculative assertion by the Tasmanian Director of Public Prosecutions near the end of her trial. There was no such wrench; in fact no murder weapon was presented as an exhibit to the court. There were no eye witnesses.

While the wrench was a suggestion by the prosecution (see below), it would have made a vivid impression in the minds of the jury. It certainly did in the mind of the judge, who referred to it eight times in his summing up, reinforcing from the bench the idea of that phantom wrench.

This is how DPP Tim Ellis speculated on how Sue murdered Bob on the boat during the trial: "It was a wrench, wasn't it, or a similar sort of tool with which you struck Mr Chappell from behind and killed him…"

"Mr Ellis, I have never struck anybody, let alone someone I loved dearly," replied Neill-Fraser.

Justice Blow referred to the imaginary wrench several times in his summing up to the jury – here are six references from the transcript of the trial:

Blow J summing up, p 1501

So, for example, if she was walking through the boat and tripped and fell and happened to be carrying a terribly heavy wrench which hit him on the back of the head causing death, that wouldn't be a voluntary and intentional act

Blow J summing up, p 1506

Mr Ellis in cross-examining Ms Neill-Fraser put to her a series of propositions, a scenario about killing Mr Chappell with a wrench, attacking him from behind, and killing him because of a difference of views about the yacht and expenditure and of the future of the yacht. Well it's not essential that you be satisfied beyond reasonable doubt as to the correctness of any or all of those propositions. You – you – it's open to you to be satisfied beyond reasonable doubt of guilt without being satisfied of particular contentions or theories as to precisely what happened or why it happened;

Blow J summing up, p 1542

And it's murder if the type of bodily harm that is intended is likely to cause death in the circumstances and the killer knows that. So let's take the example of hitting a man on the head with a wrench. If an assailant who has no wish to kill the victim hits the victim on the head with a wrench very hard you might think that that's intended –

Blow J summing up, p 1543

So if an assailant hits someone on the head with a wrench, for example, and if that sort of bodily harm that's intended, a head injury caused with a wrench, is something that could well cause death

Blow J summing up, p 1543

For example, if the assailant thinks, 'I don't care whether he dies or not, I'm so angry with him I'm going to hit him on the head with this wrench and that'll really hurt him', then that can amount to murder.

The prosecution also speculated how Sue Neill-Fraser moved the body (said to weigh 64 kilos) from below decks, up two flights of stairs, then up over the hand railing and over the side, into the bobbing dinghy, with a fire extinguisher attached. And then dumped the body from the dinghy further along the Derwent River. Alone. In the dark of night.

The judge had clearly accepted the speculation as if proven and regurgitated it in his sentencing remarks: "*I am satisfied beyond reasonable doubt that Ms Neill-Fraser used the ropes and winches on the yacht to lift Mr Chappell's body onto the deck; that she manoeuvred his body into the yacht's tender; that she attached an old-fashioned fire extinguisher weighing about 14 kilograms to his body; that she travelled away from the Four Winds in the tender with the body for some distance; and that she dumped the body in deep water somewhere in the river.*"

In fact, there was no evidence that Neill-Fraser did any of those things of which the judge was satisfied beyond reasonable doubt.

All those enabling or protecting this conviction are party to a gross miscarriage of justice in the author's opinion. They have ignored the rule of law, and participated in debasing their legal system, which will haunt Tasmania for a long time.

WHO'S WHO

As Lara Giddings says in her Foreword, many people have gathered round to support Sue Neill-Fraser in her fight to clear her name. Perhaps the earliest and arguably most passionate was **Eve Ash,** Melbourne-based award winning motivational psychologist & speaker, and founder of business video production company, Seven Dimensions. When a respected former employee, Mark Bowles, rang her in bewilderment to say his mother in law, Sue Neill-Fraser, had been arrested on a charge of murder, Eve immediately began work on a documentary. It seemed so out of character and absurd, she was sure the investigation would fizzle out. It didn't...

Since completing that documentary, Shadow of Doubt, which screened in 2013 on the CSi channel of Foxtel, she has made Undercurrent, a 6-part TV documentary series on the subject for Channel 7, and produced a 29-episode podcast, Who Killed Bob, which has had 2.3 million listeners by early 2023.

It was Shadow of Doubt, reviewed in 2013 by this author, then a film critic, that provided the motivation for Urban's online blog, wrongfulconvictionsreport.org and his book, Murder by the Prosecution, the prequel to this book.

Ash had a close working relationship with Hobart lawyer **Barbara Etter** APM, who had taken on Sue's case (pro bono) in the wake of the failed first appeal in 2011 – and after the High Court refused leave to hear her appeal in 2012. Etter, awarded the Australian Police Medal (APM) for her earlier work in the police, also spent a stint as Tasmania's Integrity Commissioner. Etter's meticulous attention to detail and her determined efforts to unearth details of the police investigation eventually led to the preparation of an extensive and damning report (quoted in this book), developed with Melbourne barrister Hugh Selby, which was tabled in Parliament by Independent MP (Mersey) Mike Gaffney MLC in August 2021. (Etter made enemies in Hobart's legal circles with her advocacy for Neill-Fraser. She no longer practices law. For a detailed report on her fight with the Legal Profession Board, please visit https://wrongfulconvictionsreport.org/2019/04/28/barbara-etter-the-facts/)

Ash also introduced the author to UK born **Dr Bob Moles**, the Flinders University legal academic well known for his expertise on miscarriages of justice, who has provided much legal guidance and analysis of the case not only for this book but its prequel and to the author's blog. He has prepared several reports on various aspects of the Sue Neill-Fraser case and considers the conviction ought to be overturned on several grounds, as outlined in this book. He was convenor of a Symposium on Miscarriages of Justice at Flinders University in November 2014.

He publishes Networked Knowledge, a resource full of analysis and case studies. An author of multiple books, some with fellow legal academic Bibi Sangha, Moles has been sought out for advice on the establishment of Canada's Criminal Cases Review Commission, among other such tasks. He graduated LLB(Hons) from Queens University, Belfast, as the top student in 1978. He completed his doctorate at the University of Edinburgh.

ANDREW L. URBAN

Since 2013, Andrew has been investigating wrongful convictions, and writing about them in *The Australian*, in his 2018 book, *Murder by the Prosecution* and now its 2023 sequel, *The Exoneration Papers - Sue Neill-Fraser* and on his blog wrongfulconvictionsreport.org

He has also had published *Zelensky – the unlikely hero, Margaret Cunneen – the boxing butterfly, Gladys – staying strong, Climate Alarm Reality Check*, and has several books in the pipeline.

His first novel, *If You Promise Not To Tell* (1995) was republished in 2019 (Wilkinson).

Andrew's career is grounded in his professional forte as an interviewer. He was the creator of *Front Up*, the 1990s prime time television program which aired on SBS for nine years, in which he fronted up to people in the streets of Australia for an impromptu conversation about their private lives. The experience taught him never to assume anything about anyone.

As a freelance journalist, Andrew has contributed (over 2,000 articles) to a wide range of publications, including The Australian (including The Weekend Australian & The Australian Colour Magazine), The Sydney Morning Herald (including Good Weekend), Sun Herald (Sydney), Herald Sun (Auckland) and previously to The Bulletin, Cinema Papers, the Qantas in-flight magazine, international publications including The Japan Times and others. Many of these articles were interview-based.

From 1985 to 1990, he was Australian Bureau Chief for Screen International and from 1990 to 2004 for Moving Pictures, both London-based international film industry publications. In 1986, he was the first accredited Australian journalist to file stories from the Cannes film festival, and went on to cover 20 Cannes festivals.

Andrew was Channel Host for the World Movies Chanel on Foxtel from April 2002 to November 2006.

In 1998 he co-edited and conducted the interviews for Edge of the Known World, the coffee table book celebrating the first 25 years of the Australian Film Television and Radio School. And in 2007, he was commissioned to conduct almost 100 on-camera interviews with film professionals for the Centre for Screen Business at the school.

He was Channel Host on the subscription tv channel, World Movies for almost 5 years and since 2005, has presented Movies Now, a contemporary film appreciation course for the Centre for Continuing Education, University of Sydney.

Andrew was publisher and editor of Australia's online movie magazine, urbancinefile.com.au, launched with his wife & partner, Louise, in 1997, which ran for 20 years.

Awards

Mardi Gras 1997 Mainstream Media Award - Front Up (SBS TV)

Best Arts & Entertainment Site 1998, Telstra/Financial Review Internet Awards, Urban Cinefile

Nominated for Best First Crime Fiction, Ned Kelly awards – If You Promise Not to Tell

HOW SUE NEILL-FRASER'S DEFENCE COUNSEL MIGHT HAVE ADDRESSED THE JURY IN SUMMING UP:

Ladies and gentlemen of the jury, I must apologise for my learned friend here, representing the Crown. He has taken you for gullible fools. He expects you to believe his fanciful speculation that this middle aged and law abiding member of our community became a murderous villain with superior strength, superior physical abilities, a sudden surge of hatred for her beloved partner Bob Chappell, which drove her to return to the Four Winds on the night of Australia Day to kill him. Just like that.

She clambered on board around midnight, my learned friend imagined, and she went down below decks, gathering a large wrench along the way, or maybe she bought it at Bunnings that afternoon without being noticed, and after saying 'Hello dear, I decided to come back after all... to kill you,' she smashed his skull from behind.

According to this hypothesis - and my learned friend has failed to offer you any proof of this - she then tied his body with rope and took the rope to the winch and hauled him up. This, too, is to be taken without evidence.

The feat of winching the body to the top deck did not exhaust her; she went on to tie a fire extinguisher to the body, although how she got this doubly bulky package through the wires and railing of the deck into the dinghy is more in the realm of miracles than of murder.

In case you were so gullible as to believe all this, my learned friend then asked you to believe the rest of his scenario in which she herself got into the dinghy - ignoring the danger of it capsizing, motored away from Four Winds and somewhere, somehow, shoved Bob Chappell's weighed-down body out of the dinghy into the Derwent, remaining safely inside the little dinghy herself . Still without evidence for any of this. Not even the dinghy's petrol consumption supports his fantasy.

Bob Chappell's body has never been found, yet the prosecutor knew what injuries would have been found on it.

He not only insulted your intelligence he broke the rules governing prosecutorial behaviour.

Your verdict of 'not guilty' will demonstrate that you are not as gullible as the prosecution thinks.

Jenny Herrera, member of the Sue Neill-Fraser Support Group.